Beautiful Stories
about
Children
by
Charles Dickens

Beautiful Stories

About

Children

By

Charles Dickens

SUPERBLY ILLUSTRATED
WITH
COLOR PLATES
AND
PEN SKETCHES

COMPILED BY MICHAEL KELSON

Bracken Books

LONDON

First published 1985
by View Productions Pty. Ltd., Sydney.

This edition published 1986 by Bracken Books,
a division of Bestseller Publications Limited, Brent House,
24 Friern Park, London N12 9DA, England.

ISBN 1 85170 006 4

Manufactured by C.T. Products, London, England.

CONTENTS

COLOR PLATES

Tiny Tim.

IT will surprise you all very much to hear that there was once a man who did not like Christmas. In fact, he had been heard on several occasions to use the word *humbug* with regard to it. His name was Scrooge, and he was a hard, sour-tempered man of business, intent only on saving and making money, and caring nothing for anyone. He paid the poor, hard-working clerk in his office as little as he could possibly get the work done for, and lived on as little as possible himself, alone, in two dismal rooms. He was never merry or comfortable or happy, and he hated other people to be so, and that was the reason why he hated Christmas, because people *will* be happy at Christmas, you know, if they possibly can, and like to have a little money to make themselves and others comfortable.

BOB CRATCHIT AND TINY TIM.

Well, it was Christmas eve, a very cold and foggy one, and Mr. Scrooge, having given his poor clerk unwilling permission to spend Christmas day at home, locked up his office and went home himself in a very bad temper, and with a cold in his head. After having taken some gruel as he sat over a miserable fire in his dismal room, he got into bed, and had some wonderful and disagreeable dreams, to which we will leave him, whilst we see how Tiny Tim, the son of his poor clerk, spent Christmas day.

The name of this clerk was Bob Cratchit. He had a wife and five other children besides Tim, who was a weak and delicate little cripple, and for this reason was dearly loved by his father and the rest of the family; not but what he was a dear little boy, too, gentle and patient and loving, with a sweet face of his own, which no one could help looking at.

Whenever he could spare the time, it was Mr. Cratchit's delight to carry his little boy out on his shoulder to see the shops and the people; and to-day he had taken him to church for the first time.

"Whatever has got your precious father and your brother Tiny Tim!" exclaimed Mrs. Cratchit, "here's dinner all ready to be dished up. I've never known him so late on Christmas day before."

"Here he is, mother!" cried Belinda, and "here he is!" cried the other children.

In came little Bob, the father, with at least three feet of comforter, exclusive of the fringe, hanging down before him; and his threadbare clothes darned up and brushed, to look seasonable; and Tiny Tim upon his shoulder. Alas for Tiny Tim, he bore a little crutch, and had his limbs supported by an iron frame!

"Why, where's our Martha?" cried Bob Cratchit, looking round.

"Not coming," said Mrs. Cratchit.

"Not coming!" said Bob, with a sudden declension in his high spirits; for he had been Tim's blood horse all the way from church, and had come home rampant. "Not coming upon Christmas day!"

Martha didn't like to see him disappointed, if it were only in joke; so she came out prematurely from behind the closet-door, and ran into his arms, while the two young Cratchits hustled Tiny Tim, and bore him off into the wash-house, that he might hear the pudding singing in the copper.

"And how did Tim behave?" asked Mrs. Cratchit.

"As good as gold and better," replied his father. "I think, wife, the child gets thoughtful, sitting at home so much. He told me, coming home, that he hoped the people in church who saw he was a cripple would be pleased to remember on Christmas day who it was who made the lame to walk."

"Bless his sweet heart!" said the mother in a trembling voice, and

TINY TIM

the father's voice trembled, too, as he remarked that "Tiny Tim was growing strong and hearty at last."

His active little crutch was heard upon the floor, and back came Tiny Tim before another word was spoken, escorted by his brother and sister to his stool beside the fire; while Bob, Master Peter, and the two ubiquitous young Cratchits went to fetch the goose, with which they soon returned in high procession.

Such a bustle ensued that you might have thought a goose the rarest of all birds; a feathered phenomenon, to which a black swan was a matter of course—and in truth it was something very like it in that house. Mrs. Cratchit made the gravy (ready beforehand in a little saucepan) hissing hot; Master Peter mashed the potatoes with incredible vigor; Miss Belinda sweetened up the apple-sauce; Martha dusted the hot plates; Bob took Tiny Tim beside him in a tiny corner at the table; the two young Cratchits set chairs for everybody, not forgetting themselves, and, mounting guard upon their posts, crammed spoons into their mouths, lest they should shriek for goose before their turn came to be helped. At last the dishes were set on, and grace was said. It was succeeded by a breathless pause, as Mrs. Cratchit, looking slowly all along the carving-knife, prepared to plunge it in the breast; but when she did, and when the long-expected gush of stuffing issued forth, one murmur of delight arose all round the board, and even Tiny Tim, excited by the two young Cratchits, beat on the table with the handle of his knife, and feebly cried Hurrah!

There never was such a goose. Bob said he didn't believe there ever was such a goose cooked. Its tenderness and flavor, size, and cheapness were the themes of universal admiration. Eked out by apple-sauce and mashed potatoes, it was a sufficient dinner for the whole family; indeed, as Mrs. Cratchit said with great delight (surveying one small atom of a bone upon the dish), they hadn't ate it all at that! Yet everyone had had enough, and the youngest Cratchits, in particular, were steeped in sage and onions to the eyebrows! But now, the plates being changed by Miss Belinda, Mrs. Cratchit left the room alone—too nervous to bear witnesses—to take the pudding up, and bring it in.

Suppose it should not be done enough! Suppose it should break in turning out! Suppose somebody should have got over the wall of the back yard and stolen it, while they were merry with the goose—a supposition at which the two young Cratchits became livid! All sorts of horrors were supposed.

Halloo! A great deal of steam! The pudding was out of the copper. A smell like a washing-day! That was the cloth. A smell like an eating-house and a pastrycook's next door to each other, with a laundress' next door to that! That was the pudding! In half a minute Mrs. Cratchit entered—flushed, but smiling proudly—with the pudding like a speckled cannon-ball, so hard and firm, blazing in half of half-a-quartern of ignited brandy, and bedight with Christmas holly stuck into the top.

Oh, a wonderful pudding! Bob Cratchit said, and calmly too, that he regarded it as the greatest success achieved by Mrs. Cratchit since their marriage. Mrs. Cratchit said that, now the weight was off her mind, she would confess she had her doubts about the quantity of flour. Everybody had something to say about it, but nobody said or thought it was at all a small pudding for a large family. It would have been flat heresy to do so. Any Cratchit would have blushed to hint at such a thing.

At last the dinner was all done, the cloth was cleared, the hearth swept, and the fire made up. The compound in the jug being tasted, and considered perfect, apples and oranges were put upon the table, and a shovel full of chestnuts on the fire. Then all the Cratchit family drew round the hearth in what Bob Cratchit called a circle, meaning half a one; and at Bob Cratchit's elbow stood the family display of glass. Two tumblers and a custard cup without a handle.

These held the hot stuff from the jug, however, as well as golden goblets would have done; and Bob served it out with beaming looks, while the chestnuts on the fire sputtered and cracked noisily. Then Bob proposed:

"A merry Christmas to us all, my dears. God bless us!"

Which all the family re-echoed.

"God bless us everyone!" said Tiny Tim, the last of all.

Now I told you that Mr. Scrooge had some disagreeble and wonderful dreams on Christmas eve, and so he had; and in one of them he dreamt that a Christmas spirit showed him his clerk's home; he saw them all gathered round the fire, and heard them drink his health, and Tiny Tim's song, and he took special note of Tiny Tim himself.

How Mr. Scrooge spent Christmas day we do not know. He may have remained in bed, having a cold, but on Christmas night he had more dreams, and the spirit took him again to his clerk's poor home. The mother was doing some needlework, seated by the table, a tear dropped on it now and then, and she said, poor thing, that the work, which was black, hurt her eyes. The children sat, sad and silent, about the room, except Tiny Tim, who was not there. Upstairs the father, with his face hidden in his hands, sat beside a little bed, on which lay a tiny figure, white and still. "My little child, my pretty little child," he sobbed, as the tears fell through his fingers on to the floor. "Tiny Tim died because his father was too poor to give him what was necessary to make him well; *you* kept him poor;" said the dream-spirit to Mr. Scrooge. The father kissed the cold, little face on the bed, and went downstairs, where the sprays of holly still remained about the humble room; and taking his hat, went out, with a wistful glance at the little crutch in the corner as he shut the door. Mr. Scrooge saw all this, and many more things as strange and sad, the spirit took care of that; but, wonderful to relate, he woke the next morning feeling a different man—feeling as he had never felt in his life before.

"Why, I am as light as a feather, and as happy as an angel, and as merry as a schoolboy," he said to himself as he absolutely skipped into the next room to breakfast and threw on all the coals at once, and put two lumps of sugar in his tea. "I hope everybody had a merry Christmas, and here's a happy New Year to all the world."

Poor Bob Cratchit crept into the office a few minutes late, expecting to be roundly abused and scolded for it, but no such thing; his master was there with his back to a good fire, and actually smiling, and he shook hands with his clerk, telling him heartily he was going to raise his salary and asking quite affectionately after Tiny Tim! "And mind you make up a good fire in your room before you set to work, Bob," he said, as he closed his own door.

Bob could hardly believe his eyes and ears, but it was all true. Such doings as they had on New Year's day had never been seen before in the Cratchits' home, nor such a turkey as Mr. Scrooge sent them for

TINY TIM.

dinner.   Tiny Tim had his share too, for Tiny Tim did not die, not a bit
of it.   Mr. Scrooge was a second father to him from that day, he wanted
for nothing, and grew up strong and hearty. Mr. Scrooge loved him, and
well he might, for was it not Tiny Tim who had unconsciously, through
the Christmas dream-spirit, touched his hard heart and caused him to
become a good and happy man?

Christmas Carol.

CRATCHIT AND MR. SCROOGE.

Little Dombey.

LITTLE DOMBEY was the son of a rich city merchant. Ever since his marriage, ten years before our story commences, Mr. Dombey had ardently desired to have a son. He was a cold, stern, and pompous man, whose life and interests were entirely absorbed in his business, which appeared to him to be the most important thing in the whole world. It was not so much that he wanted a son to love, and to love him, but because he was so desirous of having one to associate with himself in the business, and make the house once more Dombey & Son in fact, as it was in name, that the little boy who was at last born to him was so precious, and so eagerly welcomed.

There was a pretty little girl six years old, but her father had taken so little notice of her that it was doubtful if he would have known her had he met her in the street. Of what use was a girl to Dombey & Son? She could not go into the business.

Little Dombey's mother died when he was born, but the event did not greatly disturb Mr. Dombey; and since his son lived, what did it matter to him that his little daughter Florence was breaking her heart in loneliness for the mother who had loved and cherished her!

During the first few months of his life, little Dombey grew and flourished; and as soon as he was old enough to take notice, there was no one he loved so well as his sister Florence. He would laugh and hold out his arms as soon as she came in sight, and the affection of her baby brother comforted the lonely little girl, who was never weary of waiting on and playing with him.

In due time the baby was taken to

LITTLE DOMBEY AND HIS SISTER.

"He would laugh and hold out his arms as soon as she came in sight."

church, and baptized by the name of Paul (his father's name). A grand and stately christening it was, followed by a grand and stately feast; and little Paul, when he was brought in to be admired by the company, was declared by his godmother to be "an angel, and the perfect picture of his own papa."

LITTLE DOMBEY.

Whether baby Paul caught cold on his christening day or not, no one could tell, but from that time he seemed to waste and pine; his healthy and thriving babyhood had received a check, and as for illnesses, "There never was a blessed dear so put upon," his nurse said. Every tooth cost him a fit, and as for chicken-pox, whooping-cough, and measles, they followed one upon the other, and, to quote Nurse Richards again, "seized and worried him like tiger cats," so that by the time he was five years old, though he had the prettiest, sweetest little face in the world, there was always a patient, wistful look upon it, and he was thin and tiny and delicate. He would be as merry and full of spirits as other children when playing with Florence in their nursery, but he soon got tired, and had such old-fashioned ways of speaking and doing things, that Richards often shook her head sadly over him.

DOMBEY AND SON.

When he sat in his little arm-chair with his father, after dinner, as Mr. Dombey would have him do every day, they were a strange pair— so like, and so unlike each other.

"What is money, papa?" asked Paul on one of these occasions, crossing his tiny arms as well as he could—just as his father's were crossed.

16

"Why, gold, silver, and copper; you know what **it is well enough,** Paul," answered his father.

"Oh, yes; I mean, what can money do?"

"Anything, everything—almost," replied Mr. Dombey, taking one **of** his son's wee hands, and beating it softly against his own.

Paul drew his hand gently away. "It didn't save me my mamma, and it can't make me strong and big," said he.

"Why, you *are* strong and big, as big as such little people usually are," returned Mr. Dombey.

"No," replied Paul, sighing; "when Florence was as little as me, she was strong and tall, and did not get tired of playing as I do. I am *so* tired sometimes, papa."

Mr. Dombey's anxiety was aroused, and he summoned his sister, Mrs. Chick, to consult with him over Paul, and the doctor was sent for to examine him.

"The child is hardly so stout as we could wish," said the doctor; "his mind is too big for his body, he thinks too much—let him try sea-air— sea-air does wonders for children."

So it was arranged that Florence, Paul, and nurse should go to Brighton, and stay in the house of a lady named Mrs. Pipchin, who kept a very select boarding-house for children, and whose management of them was said, in the best circles, to be truly marvelous. Mr. Dombey himself went down to Brighton every week, and had the children to stay with him at his hotel from Saturday to Monday, that he might judge of the progress made by his son and heir towards health.

There is no doubt that, apart from his importance to the house of Dombey & Son, little Paul had crept into his father's heart, cold though it still was towards his daughter, colder than ever now, for there was in it a sort of unacknowledged jealousy of the warm love lavished on her by Paul, which he himself was unable to win.

Mrs. Pipchin was a marvelously ugly old lady, with a hook nose and stern cold eyes. Two other children lived at present under her charge, a mild blue-eyed little girl who was known as Miss Pankey, and a Master Bitherstone, a solemn and sad-looking little boy whose parents were in India, and who asked Florence in a depressed voice whether she could give him any idea of the way back to Bengal.

LITTLE PAUL AND FLORENCE.

THE GAME CHICKEN

"Well, Master Paul, how do you think you will like me?" said Mrs. Pipchin, seeing the child intently regarding her.

"I don't think I shall like you at all," replied Paul, shaking his head. "I want to go away. I do not like your house."

Paul did not like Mrs. Pipchin, but he would sit in his arm-chair and look at her, just as he had looked at his father at home. Her ugliness seemed to fascinate him.

As the weeks went by little Paul grew more healthy-looking, but he did not seem any stronger, and could not run about out of doors. A little carriage was therefore got for him, in which he could be wheeled down to the beach, where he would pass the greater part of the day.

Consistent in his odd tastes, the child set aside a ruddy-faced lad who was proposed as the drawer of his carriage, and selected, instead, his grandfather—a weazen, cold, crab-faced man, in a suit of battered oilskin, who had got tough and stringy from long pickling in salt water, and who smelt like a weedy seabeach when the tide is out.

With this notable attendant to pull him along, and Florence always walking by his side, and the despondent Wickam bringing up the rear, he went down to the margin of the ocean every day; and there he would sit or lie in his carriage for hours together; never so distressed as by the company of children—Florence alone excepted, always.

"Go away, if you please," he would say to any child who came to bear him company. "Thank you, but I don't want you."

Some small voice, near his ear, would ask him how he was, perhaps.

"I am very well, I thank you," he would answer. "But you had better go and play, if you please."

Then he would turn his head, and watch the child away, and say to Florence, "We don't want any others, do we? Kiss me, Floy."

"I love you, Floy," he said one day to her; "if you went to India as that boy's sister did, I should die."

Florence laid her head against his pillow, and whispered how much stronger he was growing.

"Oh yes, I know, I am a great deal better," said Paul, "a very great deal better. Listen, Floy; what is it the sea keeps saying?"

"Nothing, dear; it is only the rolling of the waves you hear."

"Yes, but they are always saying something, and always the same thing. What place is over there, Floy?"

She told him there was another country opposite, but Paul said he did not mean that, he meant somewhere much farther away, oh, much farther away—and often he would break off in the midst of their talk to listen to the sea and gaze out towards that country "farther away."

After having lived at Brighton for a year, Paul was certainly much stronger, though still thin and delicate. And on one of his weekly visits, Mr. Dombey observed to Mrs. Pipchin, with pompous condescension, "My son is getting on, Madam, he is really getting on. He is six years of age, and six will be sixteen before we have time to look about us." And then he went on to explain that Paul's weak health having kept him back in his studies, which, considering the great destiny before the heir of Dombey & Son, was much to be regretted, he had made arrangements to place him at the educational establishment of Dr. Blimber, which was close by. Florence was, for the present, to remain under Mrs. Pipchin's care, and see her brother every week.

Dr. Blimber's school was a great hot-house for the forcing of boys' brains;—no matter how backward a boy was, Doctor Blimber could always bring him on, and make a man of him in no time; and Dr. Blimber promised speedily to make a man of Paul.

"Shall you like to be made a man of, my son?" asked Mr. Dombey.

"I'd rather be a child and stay with Floy," answered Paul.

Then a different life began for little Dombey.

Miss Blimber, the doctor's daughter, a learned lady in spectacles, was his special tutor, and from morning till night his poor little brains were forced and crammed, till his head was heavy and always had a dull ache in it, and his small legs grew weak again—every day he looked a little thinner and a little paler, and became more old-fashioned than ever in his looks and ways—"old-fashioned" was a distinguishing title which clung to him. He was gentle and polite to everyone—always looking out for small kindnesses which he might do to any inmate of the house. Everyone liked "little Dombey," but everyone down to the footman said with the same kind of tender smile—he was such an old-fashioned boy. "The oddest and most old-fashioned child in the world," Dr. Blimber would say to his daughter; "but bring him on, Cornelia—bring him on."

FLORENCE AND LITTLE PAUL.

And Cornelia did bring him on; and Florence, seeing how pale and weary the little fellow looked when he came to her on Saturdays, and how he could not rest from anxiety about his lessons, would lighten his labors a little, and ease his mind by helping him to prepare his week's work.

One of Paul's friends at Dr. Blimber's school was a Mr. Toots, a young gentleman with a swollen nose and an excessively large head. The people said that the doctor overdid it with young Toots, and that when he began to have whiskers he left off having brains.

One day, when his lessons were over, about a fortnight before the commencement of holidays, little Paul's head, which had long been ailing more or less, and was sometimes very heavy and painful, felt so uneasy that night that he was obliged to support it on his hand. And yet it drooped so, that by little and little it sank on Mr. Toots' knee, and rested there, as if it had no care ever to be lifted up again.

That was no reason why he should be deaf; but he must have been, he thought, for, by-and-by, he heard Mr. Feeder calling in his ear, and gently shaking him to rouse his attention. And when he raised his head, quite scared, and looked about him, he found that Doctor Blimber had come into the room; and that the window was open, and that his forehead was wet with sprinkled water; though how all this had been done without his knowledge was very curious indeed.

"Ah! Come, come! That's well! How is my little friend now?" said Doctor Blimber, encouragingly.

"Oh, quite well, thank you, sir," said Paul.

But there seemed to be something the matter with the floor, for he couldn't stand upon it steadily; and with the walls too, for they were inclined to turn round and round, and could only be stopped by being looked at very hard indeed. Mr. Toots' head had the appearance of being at once bigger and farther off than was quite natural; and when he took Paul in his arms, to carry him up stairs, Paul observed with astonishment that the door was in quite a different place from that in which he had expected to find it, and almost thought, at first, that Mr. Toots was going to walk straight up the chimney.

It was very kind of Mr. Toots, Paul's chief patron, to carry him to the top of the house so tenderly; and Paul told him that it was. But Mr. Toots said he would do a great deal more than that, if he could; and indeed he did more as it was: for he helped Paul to undress, and helped him to bed, in the kindnest manner possible.

In a few days Paul was able to get up and creep about the house. He wondered sometimes why everyone looked at and spoke so very kindly to him, and was more than ever careful to do any little kindnesses he could think of for them: even the rough, ugly dog Diogenes, who lived in the yard, came in for a share of his attentions.

There was to be a party at Dr. Blimber's on the evening before the boys went home, and Paul wished to remain for this, because Florence was coming, and he wanted her to see how everyone was fond of him. He was to go away with her after the party. Paul sat in a corner of the sofa all the evening, and everyone was very kind to him indeed, it was quite extraordinary, Paul thought, and he was very happy; he liked to see how pretty Florence was, and how everyone admired and wished to dance with her. When the time came for them to take leave, the whole houseful gathered on the steps to say good-by to little Dombey and his sister, Toots even opening the carriage-door to say it over again.

"Good-by, Doctor Blimber," said Paul, stretching out his hand.

"Good-by, my little friend," returned the doctor.

"I'm very much obliged to you, sir," said Paul, looking innocently up into his awful face. "Ask them to take care of Diogenes, if you please."

Diogenes was the dog, who had never in his life received a friend into his confidence before Paul. So the doctor promised that every attention should be paid to Diogenes in Paul's absence.

After resting for a night at Mrs. Pipchin's house, little Paul went home, and was carried straight upstairs to his bed.

"Floy, dear," said he to his sister, when he was comfortably settled, "was that papa in the hall when I was carried in?"

"Yes, dear," answered Florence.

"He didn't cry, did he, Floy, and go into his own room when he saw me?"

Florence could only shake her head and hide her face against his, as she kissed him.

"I should not like to think papa cried," murmured little Paul, as he went to sleep.

He lay in his bed day after day quite happily and patiently, content to watch and talk to Florence. He would tell her his dreams, and how he always saw the sunlit ripples of a river rolling, rolling fast in front of him; sometimes he seemed to be rocking in a little boat on the water, and its motion lulled him to rest, and then he would be floating away, away to that shore farther off, which he could not see. One day he told Florence that the water was rippling brighter and faster than ever, and that he could not see anything else.

"My own boy, cannot you see your poor father?" said Mr. Dombey, bending over him.

"Oh yes; but don't be so sorry, dear papa, I am so happy—good-by, dear papa." Presently he opened his eyes again, and said, "Floy, mamma is like you, I can see her. Come close to me, Floy, and tell them," whispered the dying boy, "that the face of the picture of Christ on the staircase at school is not divine enough; the light from it is shining on me now, and the water is shining too, and rippling so fast, so fast."

The evening light shone into the room, but little Paul's spirit had

DEAR, GENTLE, PATIENT, NOBLE NELL

MR. PICKWICK

"MARCHIONESS" SAID MR. SWIVELLER

"JINGLE," SAID THE VERSATILE GENTLEMAN

gone out on the rippling water, and the divine face was shining on him from the farther shore.

One day, about a week after the funeral, Florence was sitting at her work, when Susan appeared, with a face half-laughing and half-crying, to announce a visitor.

"A visitor! To me, Susan!" said Florence, looking up in astonishment.

"Well, it *is* a wonder, ain't it now, Miss Floy," said Susan; "but I wish you had a many visitors, I do, indeed, for you'd be all the better for it, and it's my opinion that the sooner you and me goes even to them old Skettleses, Miss, the better for both: I may not wish to live in crowds, Miss Floy, but still I'm not an oyster."

To do Miss Nipper justice, she spoke more for her young mistress than herself; and her face showed it.

"But the visitor, Susan?" said Florence.

Susan, with an hysterical explosion, that was as much a laugh as a sob, and as much a sob as a laugh, answered:

"Mr. Toots!"

The smile that appeared on Florence's face passed from it in a moment, and her eyes filled with tears. But at any rate it was a smile, and that gave great satisfaction to Miss Nipper.

"My own feelings exactly, Miss Floy," said Susan, putting her apron to her eyes, and shaking her head. "Immediately I see that innocent in the hall, Miss Floy, I burst out laughing first, and then I choked."

Susan Nipper involuntarily proceeded to do the like again on the spot. In the meantime Mr. Toots, who had come upstairs after her, all unconscious of the effect he produced, announced himself with his knuckles on the door, and walked in very briskly.

"How d'ye do, Miss Dombey?" said Mr. Toots. "I am very well, I thank you; how are you?"

Mr. Toots—than whom there were few better fellows in the world, though there may have been one or two brighter spirits—had laboriously invented this long burst of discourse with the view of relieving the feelings both of Florence and himself. But finding that he had run through his property, as it were, in an injudicious manner, by squandering the whole before taking a chair, or before Florence had uttered a word, or before he had well got in at the door, he deemed it advisable to begin again.

"How dy'e do, Miss Dombey?" said Mr. Toots. "I'm very well, I thank you; how are you?"

Florence gave him her hand, and said she was very well.

"I'm very well, indeed," said Mr. Toots, taking a chair. "Very well, indeed, I am. I don't remember," said Mr. Toots, after reflecting a little, "that I was ever better, thank you."

"It's very kind of you to come," said Florence, taking up her work. "I am very glad to see you."

Mr. Toots replied with a chuckle. Thinking that might be too lively, he corrected it with a sigh. Thinking that might be too melancholy, he corrected it with a chuckle. Not thoroughly pleasing himself with either mode of reply, he breathed hard.

"You were very kind to my dear brother," said Florence, obeying her own natural impulse to relieve him by saying so. "He often talked to me about you."

MISS BLIMBER AND PAUL.

"Oh, it's of no consequence," said Mr. Toots, hastily. "Warm, ain't it?"

"It's beautiful weather," replied Florence.

"It agrees with *me!*" said Mr. Toots. "I don't think I ever was so well as I find myself at present, I'm obliged to you."

After stating this curious and unexpected fact, Mr. Toots fell into a deep well of silence.

"You have left Doctor Blimber's, I think?" said Florence, trying to help him out.

"I should hope so," returned Mr. Toots. And tumbled in again.

He remained at the bottom, apparently drowned, for at least ten minutes. At the expiration of that period, he suddenly floated, and said,

"Well! Good-morning, Miss Dombey."

"Are you going?" asked Florence, rising.

"I don't know, though. No, not just at present," said Mr. Toots, sitting down again, most unexpectedly. "The fact is—I say, Miss Dombey!"

"Don't be afraid to speak to me," said Florence, with a quiet smile. "I should be very glad if you would talk about my brother."

"Would you, though," retorted Mr. Toots, with sympathy in every fibre of his otherwise expressionless face. "Poor Dombey! [I'm sure I never thought that Burgess & Co.—fashionable tailors (but very dear), that we used to talk about—would make this suit of clothes for such a purpose." Mr. Toots was dressed in mourning.] "Poor Dombey! I say! Miss Dombey!" blubbered Toots.

"Yes," said Florence.

"There's a friend he took to very much at last. I thought you'd like to have him, perhaps, as a sort of keepsake. You remember his remembering Diogenes?"

"Oh yes! oh yes!" cried Florence.

"Poor Dombey! So do I," said Mr. Toots.

Mr. Toots, seeing Florence in tears, had great difficulty in getting beyond this point, and had nearly tumbled into the well again. But a chuckle saved him on the brink.

"I say," he proceeded, "Miss Dombey! I could have had him stolen for ten shillings, if they hadn't given him up: and I would: but they were glad to get rid of him, I think. If you'd like to have him, he's at the door. I brought him on purpose for you. He ain't a lady's dog, you know," said Mr. Toots, "but you won't mind that, will you?"

In fact, Diogenes was at that moment, as they presently ascertained from looking down into the street, staring through the window of a hackney cabriolet, into which, for conveyance to that spot, he had been ensnared, on a false pretense of rats among the straw. Sooth to say, he was as unlike a lady's dog as dog might be; and in his gruff anxiety to get out presented an appearance sufficiently unpromising, as he gave short yelps out of one side of his mouth, and overbalancing himself by the intensity of every one of those efforts, tumbled down into the straw, and then sprang panting up again, putting out his tongue, as if he had come express to a dispensary to be examined for his health.

But though Diogenes was as ridiculous a dog as one would meet with

"I DON'T THINK I SHALL LIKE YOU AT ALL," REPLIED PAUL.

on a summer's day; a blundering, ill-favored, clumsy, bullet-headed dog, continually acting on a wrong idea that there was an enemy in the neighborhood, whom it was meritorious to bark at; and though he was far from good-tempered, and certainly was not clever, and had hair all over his eyes, and a comic nose, and an inconsistent tail, and a gruff voice;

he was dearer to Florence, in virtue of that parting remembrance of him and that request that he might be taken care of, than the most valuable and beautiful of his kind. So dear, indeed, was this same ugly Diogenes, and so welcome to her, that she took the jeweled hand of Mr. Toots and kissed it in her gratitude. And when Diogenes, released, came tearing up the stairs and bouncing into the room, dived under all the furniture, and wound a long iron chain, that dangled from his neck, round legs of chairs and tables, and then tugged at it until his eyes became unnaturally visible, in consequence of their nearly starting out of his head; and when he growled at Mr. Toots, who affected familiarity; Florence was as pleased with him as if he had been a miracle of discretion.

Mr. Toots was so overjoyed by the success of his present, and was so delighted to see Florence bending down over Diogenes, smoothing his coarse back with her delicate little hand—Diogenes graciously allowing it from the first moment of their acquaintance—that he felt it difficult to take leave, and would, no doubt, have been a much longer time in making up his mind to do so, if he had not been assisted by Diogenes himself, who suddenly took it into his head to bay Mr. Toots, and to make short runs at him with his mouth open. Not exactly seeing his way to the end of these demonstrations, and sensible that they placed the pantaloons constructed by the art of Burgess & Co. in jeopardy, Mr. Toots, with chuckles, finally took himself off and got away.

"Come, then, Di! Dear Di! Make friends with your new mistress. Let us love each other, Di!" said Florence, fondling his shaggy head. And Di, the rough and gruff, as if his hairy hide were pervious to the tear that dropped upon it, and his dog's heart melted as it fell, put his nose up to her face, and swore fidelity.

[Diogenes the man did not speak plainer to Alexander the Great than Diogenes the dog spoke to Florence]. He subscribed to the offer of his little mistress cheerfully, and devoted himself to her service. A banquet was immediately provided for him in a corner; and when he had eaten and drunk his fill, he went to the window where Florence was sitting, looking on, rose up on his hind legs, with his awkward forepaws on her shoulders, licked her face and hands, nestled his great head against her heart, and wagged his tail till he was tired. Finally, Diogenes coiled himself up at her feet and went to sleep.

The Runaway Couple.

MASTER HARRY AND NORAH ARRIVE AT THE HOLLY-TREE INN.

"SUPPOS- ING a young gentleman not eight years old was to run away with a fine young woman of seven, would you consider that a queer start? That there is a start as I—the Boots at the Holly- Tree Inn—have seen with my own eyes; and I cleaned the shoes they ran away in, and they was so little that I couldn't get my hand into 'em.

"Master Har- ry Walmers' father, he lived at the Elms, away by Shoot- er's Hill, six or seven miles from London. He was uncommon proud of Master Harry, as he was his only child ; but he didn't spoil him neither. He was a gentleman that had a will of his own, and an eye of his own, and that would be minded. Consequently, though he made quite a companion of the fine bright boy, still he kept the command over him, and the child *was* a child. I was under-gardener there at that time ; and one morning Master Harry, he comes to me and says—

"'Cobbs, how should you spell Norah, if you was asked ?' and then begun cutting it in print, all over the fence.

"He couldn't say he had taken particular notice of children before that ; but really it was pretty to see them two mites a-going about the place together, deep in love. And the courage of the boy ! Bless your soul, he'd have throwed off his little hat, and tucked up his little sleeves, and gone in at a lion, he would, if they had happened to meet one and she had been frightened of him. One day he stops along, with her, where Boots was hoeing weeds in the gravel, and says—speaking up, 'Cobbs,' he says, 'I like you.' 'Do you, sir ? I'm proud to hear it.' 'Yes, I do, Cobbs. Why do I like you, do you think, Cobbs ?' 'Don't know, Master Harry, I am sure.' 'Because Norah likes you, Cobbs.' 'Indeed, sir ? That's very gratifying.' 'Gratifying, Cobbs ? It's better than millions of the brightest diamonds to be liked by Norah.' 'Certainly, sir.' 'You're going away, ain't you, Cobbs ?' 'Yes, sir.' 'Would you like another situation, Cobbs ?' 'Well, sir, I shouldn't object, if it was a good 'un.' 'Then, Cobbs,' says he, 'you shall be our head-gardener when we are married.' And he tucks her, in her little sky-blue mantle, under his arm, and walks away.

"It was better than a picter, and equal to a play, to see them babies with their long, bright, curling hair, their sparkling eyes, and their beautiful light tread, a-rambling about the garden, deep in love. Boots was of opinion that the birds believed they was birds, and kept up with 'em, singing to please 'em. Sometimes, they would creep under the Tulip tree, and would sit there with their arms round one another's necks, and their soft cheeks touching, a-reading about the prince and the dragon, and the good and bad enchanters, and the king's fair daughter. Sometimes he would hear them planning about having a house in a forest, keeping bees and a cow, and living entirely on milk and honey. Once he came upon them by the pond, and heard Master

Harry say, 'Adorable Norah, kiss me, and say you love me to distraction, or I'll jump in headforemost.' And Boots made no question he would have done it, if she hadn't complied.

" 'Cobbs,' says Master Harry, one evening, when Cobbs was watering the flowers, 'I am going on a visit, this present mid-summer, to my grandmamma's at York.'

" 'Are you, indeed, sir? I hope you'll have a pleasant time. I am going into Yorkshire myself when I leave here.'

" 'Are you going to your grandmamma's, Cobbs?'

" 'No, sir. I haven't got such a thing.'

" 'Not as a grandmamma, Cobbs?'

" 'No, sir.'

" The boy looked on at the watering of the flowers for a little while and then said, 'I shall be very glad, indeed, to go, Cobbs — Norah's going.'

" 'You'll be all right then, sir,' says Cobbs, 'with your beautiful sweetheart by your side.'

" 'Cobbs,' returned the boy, flushing, 'I never let anybody joke about it when I can prevent them.'

" 'It wasn't a joke, sir,' says Cobbs, with humility— 'wasn't so meant.'

" 'I am glad of that, Cobbs, because I like you, you know, and you're going to live with us. Cobbs!'

" 'Sir.'

" 'What do you think my grandmamma gives me, when I go down there?'

MASTER HARRY AND NORAH.
"Walks into the house much bolder than brass."

" ' I couldn't so much as make a guess, sir.'

" ' A Bank of England five-pound note, Cobbs.'

" ' Whew ! ' says Cobbs, 'that's a spanking sum of money, Master Harry.'

" ' A person could do a great deal with such a sum of money as that. Couldn't a person, Cobbs ? '

" ' I believe you, sir ! '

" ' Cobbs,' said the boy, 'I'll tell you a secret.   At Norah's house they have been joking her about me, and pretending to laugh at our being engaged.   Pretending to make game of it, Cobbs ! '

" ' Such, sir,' says Cobbs, ' is the depravity of human natur'.'

" The boy, looking exactly like his father, stood for a few minutes with his glowing face towards the sunset, and then departed with, ' Good-night, Cobbs.   I'm going in.'

" I was the Boots at the Holly-Tree Inn when one summer afternoon the coach drives up, and out of the coach gets these two children.

" The guard says to our governor, ' I don't quite make out these little passengers, but the young gentleman's words was, that they were to be brought here.'   The young gentleman gets out ; hands his lady out ; gives the guard something for himself ; says to our governor, ' We're to stop here to-night, please.   Sitting-room and two bedrooms will be required. Chops and cherry-pudding for two ! '   and tucks her, in her little sky-blue mantle, under his arm, and walks into the house much bolder than brass.

" Boots leaves me to judge what the amazement of that establishment was when those two tiny creatures, all alone by themselves, was marched into the Angel—much more so when he, who had seen them without their seeing him, give the governor his views of the expedition they was upon.   ' Cobbs,' says the governor, ' if this is so, I must set off myself to York and quiet their friends' minds.   In which case you must keep your eye upon 'em, and humor 'em, till I come back.   But, before I take these measures, Cobbs, I should wish you to find out from themselves whether your opinions is correct.'   ' Sir to you,' says Cobbs, ' that shall be done directly.'

" So Boots goes up stairs to the Angel, and there he finds Master Harry on an enormous sofa a-drying the eyes of Miss Norah with his pocket-hankecher. Their little legs were entirely off the ground of course, and it really is not possible for Boots to express to me how small them children looked.

"'It's Cobbs! It's Cobbs!' cries Master Harry, and comes running to him, and catching hold of his hand. Miss Norah comes running to him on t'other

"And they laid down on a bank of daisies and fell asleep."

side, and catching hold of his t'other hand, and they both jump for joy.

"'I see you a-getting out, sir,' says Cobbs. 'I thought it was you. I thought I couldn't be mistaken in your height and figure. What's the object of your journey, sir?—Matrimonial?'

"'We are going to be married, Cobbs, at Gretna Green,' returned the boy. 'We have run away on purpose. Norah has been in rather low spirits, Cobbs; but she'll be happy, now we have found you to be our friend.'

"'Thank you, sir, and thank *you*, miss,' says Cobbs, 'for your good opinion. *Did* you bring any luggage with you, sir?'

"If I will believe Boots when he gives me his word and honor upon it, the lady had got a parasol, a smelling-bottle, a round and a half of cold buttered toast, eight peppermint drops, and a hair-brush—seemingly a doll's. The gentleman had got about half a dozen yards of string, a knife, three or four sheets of writing-paper folded up surprisingly small, an orange, and a Chaney mug with his name upon it.

"'What may be the exact natur' of your plans, sir?' says Cobbs.

"'To go on,' replied the boy—which the courage of that boy was something wonderful!—'in the morning, and be married to-morrow.'

"'Just so, sir,' says Cobbs. 'Would it meet your views, sir, if I was to accompany you?'

"When Cobbs said this, they both jumped for joy again, and cried out, 'Oh, yes, yes, Cobbs! Yes!'

"'Well, sir,' says Cobbs. 'If you will excuse my having the freedom to give an opinion, what I should recommend would be this. I'm acquainted with a pony, sir, which, put in a phaeton that I could borrow, would take you and Mrs. Harry Walmers, Jr. (myself driving, if you approve), to the end of your journey in a very short space of time. I am not altogether sure, sir, that this pony will be at liberty to-morrow, but even if you had to wait over to-morrow for him, it might be worth your while. As to the small account here, sir, in case you was to find yourself running at all short, that don't signify, because I'm a part proprietor of this inn, and it could stand over.'

"Boots assures me that when they clapped their hands and jumped for joy again, and called him, 'Good Cobbs!' and 'Dear Cobbs!' and bent across him to kiss one another in the delight of their confiding hearts, he felt himself the meanest rascal for deceiving 'em that ever was born.

"'Is there anything you want just at present, sir?' says Cobbs, mortally ashamed of himself.

"'We would like some cakes after dinner,' answered Master Harry, folding his arms, putting out one leg, and looking straight at him, 'and two apples—and jam. With dinner, we should like to have toast and water. But Norah has always been accustomed to half a glass of currant wine at dessert. And so have I.'

"'It shall be ordered at the bar, sir,' says Cobbs; and away he went.

"The way in which the women of that house—without exception—everyone of 'em—married and single, took to that boy when they heard the story, Boots considers surprising. It was as much as he could do to keep 'em from dashing into the room and kissing him. They climbed up all sorts of places, at the risk of their lives, to look at him through a pane of glass. They were seven deep at the key-hole. They were out of their minds about him and his bold spirit.

"In the evening Boots went into the room, to see how the runaway couple was getting on. The gentleman was on the window-seat, supporting the lady in his arms. She had tears upon her face, and was lying, very tired and half-asleep, with her head upon his shoulder.

THE RUNAWAY COUPLE.

" 'Mrs. Harry Walmers, Jr., fatigued, sir?' says Cobbs.

" 'Yes, she is tired, Cobbs; but she is not used to be away from home, and she has been in low spirits again. Cobbs, do you think you could bring a biffin, please?'

" 'I ask your pardon, sir, says Cobbs. 'What was it you——'

" 'I think a Norfolk biffin would rouse her, Cobbs. She is very fond of them.'

" Boots withdrew in search of the required restorative, and, when he brought it in, the gentleman handed it to the lady, and fed her with a spoon, and took a little himself. The lady being heavy with sleep, and rather cross, 'What should you think, sir,' says Cobbs, 'of a chamber candlestick?' The gentleman approved; the chambermaid went first, up the great staircase; the lady, in her sky-blue mantle, followed, gallantly escorted by the gentleman; the gentleman embraced her at the door, and retired to his own apartment, where Boots softly locked him up.

" Boots couldn't but feel what a base deceiver he was when they asked him at breakfast (they had ordered sweet milk-and-water, and toast and currant jelly, overnight) about the pony. It really was as much as he could do, he don't mind confessing to me, to look them two young things in the face, and think how wicked he had grown up to be. Howsomever, he went on a-lying like a Trojan, about the pony. He told 'em it did so unfortunately happen that the pony was half-clipped, you see, and that he couldn't be taken out in that state for fear that it should strike to his inside. But that he'd be finished clipping in the course of the day, and that to-morrow morning at eight o'clock the phaeton would be ready. Boots' view of the whole case, looking back upon it in my room, is, that Mrs. Harry Walmers, Jr., was beginning to give in. She hadn't had her hair curled when she went to bed, and she didn't seem quite up to brushing it herself, and it's getting in her eyes put her out. But nothing put out Master Harry. He sat behind his breakfast cup, a-tearing away at the jelly, as if he had been his own father.

" After breakfast Boots is inclined to consider that they drawed soldiers—at least, he knows that many such was found in the fireplace, all on horseback. In the course of the morning Master Harry rang the bell—it was surprising how that there boy did carry on—and said in a

AT THE HOLLY–TREE INN

"The lady followed, gallantly escorted by the gentleman."

sprightly way, 'Cobbs, is there any good walks in this neighborhood?'

"'Yes, sir,' says Cobbs. 'There's Love Lane.'

"'Get out with you, Cobbs!'—that was that there boy's expression—'you're joking.'

"'Begging your pardon, sir,' says Cobbs, 'there really is Love Lane. And a pleasant walk it is, and proud I shall be to show it to yourself and Mrs. Harry Walmers, Jr.'

"'Norah, dear,' said Master Harry, 'this is curious. We really ought to see Love Lane. Put on your bonnet, my sweetest darling, and we will go there with Cobbs.'

"Boots leaves me to judge what a beast he felt himself to be, when that young pair told him, as they all three jogged along together, that they had made up their minds to give him two thousand guineas a year as head-gardener, on account of his being so true a friend to 'em. Boots could have wished at the moment that the earth would have opened and swallowed him up; he felt so mean with their beaming eyes a-looking at him, and believing him. Well, sir, he turned the conversation as well as he could, and he took 'em down Love Lane to the water-meadows, and there Master Harry would have drowned himself in half a moment more, a-getting out a water-lily for her—but nothing daunted that boy. Well, sir, they was tired out. All being so new and strange to 'em, they was tired as tired could be. And they laid down on a bank of daisies, like the children in the wood, leastways meadows, and fell asleep.

"Well, sir, they woke up at last, and then one thing was getting pretty clear to Boots, namely, that Mrs. Harry Walmers', Jr., temper was on the move. When Master Harry took her round the waist she said he 'teased her so,' and when he says, 'Norah, my young May Moon, your Harry tease you?' she tells him, 'Yes; and I want to go home!'

"However, Master Harry he kept up, and his noble heart was as fond as ever. Mrs. Walmers turned very sleepy about dusk and began to cry. Therefore, Mrs. Walmers went off to bed as per yesterday; and Master Harry ditto repeated.

"About eleven or twelve at night comes back the governor in a chaise, along with Mr. Walmers and an elderly lady. Mr. Walmers looks amused and very serious, both at once, and says to our missis, 'We are very much indebted to you, ma'am, for your kind care of our little children, which we can never sufficiently acknowledge. Pray, ma'am, where is my boy?' Our missis says, 'Cobbs has the dear children in charge, sir. Cobbs, show forty!' Then he says to Cobbs, 'Ah, Cobbs! I am glad to see *you*. I understood you was here!' And Cobbs says, 'Yes, sir. Your most obedient, sir.'

"I may be surprised to hear Boots say it, perhaps, but Boots assures me that his heart beat like a hammer, going upstairs. 'I beg your pardon, sir,' says he, while unlocking the door; 'I hope you are not angry with Master Harry. For Master Harry is a fine boy, sir, and will do you credit and honor.' And Boots signifies to me that if the fine boy's father had contradicted him in the daring state of mind in which he then was, he thinks he should have 'fetched him a crack,' and taken the consequences.

"But Mr. Walmers only says, 'No, Cobbs. No, my good fellow. Thank you!' And the door being open, goes in.

"Boots goes in too, holding the light, and he sees Mr. Walmers go up to the bedside, bend gently down, and kiss the little sleeping face. Then he stands looking at it for a minute, looking wonderfully like it; and then he gently shakes the little shoulder.

"'Harry, my dear boy! Harry!'

"Master Harry starts up and looks at him. Looks at Cobbs, too.

Such is the honor of that mite that he looks at Cobbs to see whether he has brought him into trouble.

" 'I am not angry, my child. I only want you to dress yourself and come home.

" 'Yes, pa.'

"Master Harry dresses himself quickly. His breast begins to swell when he has nearly finished, and it swells more and more as he stands a-looking at his father; his father standing a-looking at him, the quiet image of him.

" 'Please may I'—the spirit of that little creatur', and the way he kept his rising tears down!—'Please, dear pa—may I—kiss Norah before I go?'

" 'You may, my child.'

"So he takes Master Harry in his hand, and Boots leads the way with the candle, and they come to that other bedroom; where the elderly lady is seated by the bed, and poor little Mrs. Harry Walmers, Jr., is fast asleep. There the father lifts the child up to the pillow, and he lays his little face down for an instant by the little warm face of poor unconscious little Mrs. Harry Walmers, Jr., and gently draws it to him— a sight so touching to the chambermaids who are peeping through the door that one of them calls out, 'It's a shame to part 'em!' But this chambermaid was always, as Boots informs me, a soft-hearted one. Not that there was any harm in that girl. Far from it."

Poor Jo!

JO AND THE BEADLE.

JO was a crossing-sweeper; his crossing was in Holborn, and there every day he swept up the mud, and begged for pennies from the people who passed. Poor Jo wasn't at all pleasant to look at. He wasn't pretty and he wasn't clean. His clothes were only a few poor rags that hardly protected him from the cold and the rain. He had never been to school, and he could neither write nor read—could not even spell his own name. He had only one name, Jo, and that served him for Christian and surname too.

Poor Jo! He was ugly and dirty and ignorant; but he knew one thing, that it was wicked to tell a lie, and knowing this, he always told the truth. One other thing poor Jo knew too well, and that was what being hungry means. For little Jo was very poor. He lived in Tom-all-Alones, one of the most horrible places in all London. The road here is thick with mud. The crazy houses are dropping away; two of them, Jo remembered, once fell to pieces. The air one breathes here is full of fever. The people who live in this dreadful den are the poorest of London poor. All miserably clad, all dirty, all very hungry. They know and like Jo, for he is always willing to go on errands for them, and does them **many little acts of kindness.** **Not that they speak of him as Jo.**

Oh, dear no! No one in Tom-all-Alones is spoken of by his name, whether it be his surname, or that which his godfathers and godmothers —always supposing that he had any—gave him. The ladies and gentlemen who live in this unfashionable neighborhood have their fashions just as much as the great folks who live in the grand mansions in the West End. Here one of the prevailing customs is to give everyone a nickname. Thus it is that if you inquired there for a boy named Jo, you would be asked whether you meant Carrots, or the Colonel, or Gallows, or young Chisel, or Terrier Tip, or Lanky, or the Brick.

Jo was generally called Toughy, although a few superior persons who gave themselves airs and graces, and affected a dignified style of speaking, called him "the tough subject."

Jo used to say he had never had but one friend.

It was one cold winter night, when he was shivering in a doorway near his crossing, that a dark-haired, rough-bearded man turned to look at him, and then came back and began to talk to him.

"Have you a friend, boy?" he asked presently.

"No, never 'ad none."

"Neither have I. Not one. Take this, and good-night," and so saying, the man who looked very poor and shabby put into Jo's hand the price of a supper and a night's lodging.

Often afterwards the stranger would stop to talk with Jo, and give him money, Jo firmly believed, whenever he had any to give. When he had none, he would merely say, "I am as poor as you are to-day, Jo," and pass on.

One day Jo was fetched away from his crossing by the beadle, and taken by him to the Sol's Arms, a public house in a little court near Chancery Lane, where the Coroner was holding an inquest—an "inkwich" Jo called it.

"Did the boy know the deceased?" asked the Coroner.

Indeed Jo had known him; it was his only friend who was dead.

"He was very good to me, he was," was all poor Jo could say.

The next day they buried the dead man in the churchyard hard by; a churchyard hemmed in by houses on either side, and separated by an iron gate from the wretched court through which one goes to it.

But that night there came a slouching figure through the court to the iron gate.   It held the gate with both hands and looked between the bars—stood looking in for a little while, then with an old broom it softly swept the step and made the archway clean.   It was poor Jo; and as,

JO AND HIS FRIEND.

after one more long look through the bars of the gate, he went away, he softly said to himself, "He was very good to me, he was."

Now, there happened to be at the inquest a kind-hearted little man named Snagsby, who was a stationer by trade, and he pitied Jo so much that he gave him half-a-crown. Half-a-crown was **Mr.** Snagsby's one remedy for all the troubles of this world.

Jo was very sad after the death of his one friend. The more so as his friend had died in great poverty and misery, with no one near him to care whether he lived or not.

It was a few days after the funeral, while Jo was still living on **Mr.** Snagsby's half-crown—half a bill, Jo called it—that a much bigger slice of good-luck fell to his share. He was standing at his crossing as the day closed in, when a lady, closely veiled and plainly dressed, came up to him.

"Are you the boy Jo who was examined at the inquest?" she asked.

"That's me," said Jo.

"Come farther up the court, I want to speak to you."

"Wot, about him as was dead? Did you know him?"

"How dare you ask me if I knew him?"

"No offense, my lady," said Jo humbly.

"Listen and hold your tongue. Show me the place where he lived, then where he died, then where they buried him. Go in front of me, don't look back once, and I'll pay you well."

"I'm fly," said Jo. "But no larks, yer know. Stow hooking it."

Jo takes her to each of the places she wants to see, and he notices that when he shows her the burying-place she shrinks into a dark corner as if to hide herself while she looks at the spot where the dead man's body rests. Then she draws off her glove, and Jo sees that she has sparkling rings on her fingers. She drops a coin into his hand and is gone. Jo holds the coin to the light and sees to his joy that it is a golden sovereign. He bites it to make sure that it is genuine, and being satisfied that it has successfully stood the test, he puts it under his tongue for safety, and goes off to Tom-all Alones.

JO AT THE GATE OF THE CHURCH-YARD WHERE THEY BURIED HIS FRIEND.

But people in Jo's position in life find it hard to change a sovereign, for who will believe that they can come by it honestly? So poor little Jo didn't get much of the sovereign for himself, for, as he afterwards told Mr. Snagsby—

"I had to pay five bob down in Tom-all-Alones before they'd square it for to give me change, and then a young man he thieved another five while I was asleep, and a boy he thieved ninepence, and the landlord he stood drains round with a lot more of it."

And so Jo was left alone in the world again, now his friend was dead. And this poor friend had only two mourners, Jo the crossing-sweeper and the lady who had come to look at his grave.

Jo mourned for him because he had been his only friend, and the lady mourned for the poor man because she had loved him dearly many years ago when they had both been young together.

As time went on Jo's troubles began in earnest. The police turned him away from his crossing, and wheresoever they met him ordered him "to move on." It was hard, very hard on poor Jo; for he knew no way of getting a living except at his crossing. So he would go back to it as often as he dared, until the police turned him away again. Once a policeman, angry to find that Jo hadn't moved on, seized him by the arm and dragged him down to Mr. Snagsby's.

"What's the matter, constable," asked Mr. Snagsby.

"This boy's as obstinate a young gonoph as I know: although repeatedly told to, he won't move on."

"I'm always a-moving on," cried Jo. "Oh, my eye, where am I to move to?"

"My instructions don't go to that," the constable answered; "my instructions are that you're to keep moving on. Now the simple question is, sir," turning to Mr. Snagsby, "whether you know him. He says you do."

"Yes, I know him."

"Very well, I leave him here; but mind you keep moving on."

The constable then moved on himself, leaving Jo at Mr. Snagsby's. There was a little tea-party there that evening, and one of the guests, a very greasy, oily-looking man, whom they called Mr. Chadband, and who was a dissenting minister, having by this time eaten and drunk a great

45

deal more than was good for him, determined to improve the occasion by delivering a discourse on Jo. It was very long and very dull to Jo: all he could remember of the sermon was this couplet—

> " O running stream of sparkling joy,
> To be a soaring human boy."

What he remembered better was, when the perspiring Chadband had finished, and he was at last allowed to go, Mr. Snagsby followed him to the door and filled his hands with the remains of the little feast they had had upstairs.

And now Jo began to find life harder and rougher than ever. He lost his crossing altogether, and spent day after day in moving on. He grew hungrier and thinner, and at last the foul air of Tom-all-Alones began to have an ill-effect even on him—"the tough subject." His throat grew very dry, his cheeks were burning hot, and his poor little head ached till the pain made him cry. Then he remembered a poor woman he had once done a kindness to, a brickmaker's wife, who had told him she lived at St. Albans, and that a lady there had been very good to her. "Perhaps she'll be good to me," thought Jo, and he started off to go to St. Albans.

So it came about that one Saturday night, Jo reached that town very tired and very ill. Happily for him the brickmaker's wife met him and took him into her cottage. While he was resting there a lady came in.

The lady sat down by the bed, and asked him very kindly what was the matter.

" I'm a-being froze and then burnt up, and then froze and burnt up again, ever so many times over in an hour. And my head's all sleepy, and all a-going round like, and I'm so dry, and my bones is nothing half so much bones as pain."

" Where are you going? "

" Somewheres," replied Jo; " I'm a-being moved on, I am."

" Well, to-night you must come with me, and I'll make you comfortable." So Jo went with the lady to a great house not far off, and there in a nice warm loft they made a bed for him, and brought him tempting wholesome food. Everyone was very kind to him, even the servants called him " Old Chap," and told him he would soon be well. Jo was really happy, and for a time forgot his pain and fever. But something frightened Jo, and he felt he could not stay there, and he ran out into the cold night-air. Where he went he could never remember, for when

he next came to his
himself in an hospital.
for some weeks, and was
though still weak and
thin, and when he
chest was very painful.
Jo, "as heavy as a
Now a certain young
name of Allan Wood-
count the hours on
takes a stroll on Tom-
morning. The banks
channel of mud is the
Tom-all-Alones, nothing
the crazy houses, shut
No waking creature save

senses he found
He stayed there
then discharged,
ill. He was very
drew a breath his
"It draws," said
cart."
doctor by the
court, rather than
a restless pillow,
all - Alones one
of a stagnant
main street of
is to be seen but
up and silent.
himself ap-
pears, ex-
cept in one
direction

POOR JO, THE CROSSING-SWEEPER.

where he sees the solitary figure of a woman sitting on a doorstep. He walks that way. Approaching, he observes that she has journeyed a long distance, and is footsore and travel-stained. She sits on the door-step in the manner of one who is waiting, with her elbow on her knee and her head upon her hand. Beside her is a canvas bag, or bundle, she has carried. She is dozing probably, for she gives no heed to his steps as he comes towards her.

The broken footway is so narrow that, when the doctor comes to where the woman sits, he has to turn into the road to pass her. Looking down at her face, his eye meets hers, and he stops.

"What is the matter?"

"Nothing, sir."

"Can't you make them hear? Do you want to be let in?"

"I'm waiting till they get up at another house—a lodging-house—not here," the woman patiently returns. "I'm waiting here because there will be sun here presently to warm me."

"I am afraid you are tired. I am sorry to see you sitting in the street."

"Thank you, sir. It don't matter."

"I suppose you have some settled home? Is it far from here?" he asks, good-humoredly making light of what he has done, as she gets up and courtesies.

"It's a good two or three-and-twenty mile from here, sir. At Saint Albans. Do you know Saint Albans, sir? I thought you gave a start like, as if you did?"

"Yes, I know something of it. And now I will ask you a question in return. Have you money for your lodging?"

"Yes, sir," she says, "really and truly." And she shows it. He tells her, in acknowledgment of her many subdued thanks, that she is very welcome, gives her good-day, and walks away. Tom-all-Alones is still asleep, and nothing is astir.

"Yes, something is! As he retraces his way to the point from which he saw the woman at a distance sitting on the step, he sees a ragged figure coming very carefully along, crouching close to the soiled walls—which the wretchedest figure might as well avoid—and thrusting a hand before it. It is the figure of a boy, whose face is hollow, and whose eyes have an emaciated glare. He is so intent on getting along unseen, that even the appearance of a stranger in whole garments does not tempt him to look back. He shades his face with his ragged elbow as he passes on the other side of the way, and goes shrinking and creeping on, with his anxious hand before him, and his shapeless clothes hanging in shreds.

Clothes made for what purpose, or of what material, it would be impossible to say. They look, in color and in substance, like a bundle of rank leaves of swampy growth, that rotted long ago.

Allan Woodcourt pauses to look after him and note all this, with a shadowy belief that he has seen the boy before. He cannot recall how, or where; but there is some association in his mind with such a form. He imagines that he must have seen it in some hospital or refuge; still, cannot make out why it comes with any special force on his remembrance.

He is gradually emerging from Tom-all-Alones in the morning light, thinking about it, when he hears running feet behind him; and looking round, sees the boy scouring towards him at great speed, followed by the woman.

"Stop him, stop him!" cries the woman almost breathless. "Stop him, sir!"

He darts across the road into the boy's path, but the boy is quicker than he—makes a curve—ducks—dives under his hands—comes up half-a-dozen yards beyond him, and scours away again. Still, the woman follows, crying, "Stop him, sir; pray stop him!" Allan, not knowing but that he has just robbed her of her money, follows in chase, and runs so hard that he runs the boy down nearly a dozen times; but each time he repeats the curve, the duck, the dive, and scours away again. To strike at him, on any of these occasions, would be to fell and disable him; but the pursuer cannot resolve to do that; and so the grimly ridiculous pursuit continues. At last the fugitive, hard-pressed, takes to a narrow passage and a court which has no thoroughfare. Here, against a hoarding of decaying timber, he is brought to bay, and tumbles down, lying gasping at his pursuer, who stands and gasps at him until the woman comes up.

"O you Jo!" cries the woman. "What? I have found you at last!"

"Jo," repeats Allan, looking at him with attention. "Jo! Stay. To be sure! I recollect this lad some time ago being brought before the Coroner."

"Yes, I see you once afore at the inkwich," whimpers Jo. "What of that? Can't you never let such an unfortnet as me alone? An't I unfortnet enough for you yet? How unfortnet do you want me fur to be? I've been a-chivied and a-chivied, fust by one on you and nixt by another on you, till I'm worrited to skins and bones. The inkwich warn't *my* fault. *I* done nothink. He wos wery good to me, he wos; he wos the only one I knowed to speak to, as ever come across my crossing. It an't wery likely I should want him to be inkwich'd. I only wish I wos, myself. I don't know why I don't go and make a hole in the water, I'm sure I don't."

He says it with such a pitiable air, and his grimy tears appear so real, and he lies in the corner up against the hoarding so like a growth of fungus, or any unwholesome excrescence produced there in neglect and impurity, that Allan Woodcourt is softened towards him. He says to the woman, "Miserable creature, what has he done?"

To which she only replies, shaking her head at the prostrate figure more amazedly than angrily: "O you Jo, you Jo. I have found you at last!"

"What has he done?" says Allan. "Has he robbed you?"

"No, sir, no. Robbed me? He did nothing but what was kind-hearted by me, and that's the wonder of it."

Allan looks from Jo to the woman, and from the woman to Jo, waiting for one of them to unravel the riddle.

"But he was along with me, sir," says the woman—"O you Jo!—he was along with me, sir, down at Saint Albans, ill, and a young lady, Lord bless her for a good friend to me, took pity on him when I durstn't, and took him home—"

Allan shrinks back from him with a sudden horror.

"Yes, sir, yes. Took him home, and made him comfortable, and like a thankless monster he ran away in the night, and never has been seen or heard of since, till I set eyes on him just now. And that young lady that was such a pretty dear caught his illness, lost her beautiful looks, and wouldn't hardly be known for the same young lady now, if it wasn't for her angel temper, and her pretty shape, and her sweet voice. Do you know it? You ungrateful wretch, do you know that this is all along of you and of her goodness to you?" demands the woman, beginning to rage at him as she recalls it, and breaking into passionate tears.

The boy, in rough sort stunned by what he hears, falls to smearing his dirty forehead with his dirty palm, and to staring at the ground, and

"I'M ALWAYS A MOVING ON!"

to shaking from head to foot until the hoarding against which he leans rattles.

Allan restrains the woman, merely by a quiet gesture, but effectually.

"You hear what she says. But get up, get up!"

Jo, shaking and chattering, slowly rises, and stands, after the manner of his tribe in a difficulty, sideways against the hoarding, resting one of his high shoulders against it, and covertly rubbing his right hand over his left, and his left foot over his right.

"You hear what she says, and I know it's true. Have you been here ever since?"

"Wishermaydie if I seen Tom-all-Alones till this blessed morning," replies Jo, hoarsely.

"Why have you come here now?"

Jo looks all round the confined court, looks at his questioner no higher than the knees, and finally answers:

"I don't know how to do nothink, and I can't get nothink to do. I'm wery poor and ill, and I thought I'd come back here when there warn't nobody about, and lay down and hide somewheres as I knows on till arter dark, and then go and beg a trifle of Mr. Snagsby. He wos allus willin' fur to give me somethink, he wos, though Mrs. Snagsby she wos allus a-chivying on me—like everybody everywheres."

"Where have you come from?"

Jo looks all round the court again, looks at his questioner's knees again, and concludes by laying his profile against the hoarding in a sort of resignation.

"Did you hear me ask you where you have come from?"

"Tramp then," says Jo.

"Now, tell me," proceeds Allan, making a strong effort to overcome his repugnance, going very near to him, and leaning over him with an expression of confidence, "tell me how it came about that you left that house, when the good young lady had been so unfortunate as to pity you, and take you home."

Jo suddenly comes out of his resignation, and excitedly declares, addressing the woman, that he never known about the young lady, that he never heern about it, that he never went fur to hurt her, that he would sooner have hurt his own self, that he'd sooner have had his unfortnet 'ead chopped off than ever gone a-nigh her, and that she wos wery good to him, she wos. Conducting himself throughout as if in his poor fashion he really meant it, and winding up with some very miserable sobs.

Allan Woodcourt sees that this is not a sham. He constrains himself to touch him. "Come, Jo. Tell me?"

"No. I dustn't," says Jo, relapsing into the profile state. "I dustn't, or I would."

"But I must know," returns the other, "all the same. Come, Jo."

After two or three such adjurations, Jo lifts up his head again, looks round the court again, and says in a low voice, "Well, I'll tell you some-think. I was took away. There!"

"Took away? In the night?"

"Ah!" Fearful of being overheard, Jo looks about him, and even glances up some ten feet at the top of the hoarding, and through the cracks in it, lest the object of his distrust should be looking over, or hidden on the other side.

"Who took you away?"

"I dustn't name him," says Jo. "I dustn't do it, sir."

"But I want, in the young lady's name, to know. You may trust me. No one else shall hear."

"Ah, but I don't know," replies Jo, shaking his head fearfully, "as he *don't* hear."

"Why, he is not in this place."

"Oh, ain't he though?" says Jo. "He's in all manner of places, all at wunst."

Allan looks at him in perplexity, but discovers some real meaning and good faith at the bottom of this bewildering reply. He patiently awaits an answer; and Jo, more baffled by his patience than by anything else, at last desperately whispers a name in his ear.

"Ay!" says Allan. "Why, what had you been doing?"

"Nothink, sir. Never done nothink to get myself into no trouble, 'sept in not moving on and the inkwich. But I'm a-moving on now. I'm a-moving on to the berryin ground—that's the move as I'm up to."

"No, no, we will try to prevent that. But what did he **do** with you?"

"Put me in a horsepittle," replied Jo, whispering, "till I wos discharged, then giv' me a little money—four half-bulls, wot you may call half-crowns—and ses 'Hook it! Nobody wants you here,' he ses. 'You hook it. You go and tramp,' he ses. 'You move on,' he ses. 'Don't let me ever see you nowheres within forty mile of London, or you'll repent it.' So I shall, if ever he does see me, and he'll see me if I'm above ground," concludes Jo, nervously repeating all his former precautions and investigations.

Allan considers a little; then says, turning to the woman, but keeping an encouraging eye on Jo: "He is not so ungrateful as you supposed. He had a reason for going away, though it was an insufficient one."

"Thank'ee, sir, thank'ee!" exclaims Jo. "There now! See how hard you wos upon me. But only you tell the young lady wot the genlmn ses, and it's all right. For *you* wos wery good to me, too, and I knows it."

"Now, Jo," says Allan, keeping his eye upon him, "come with me, and I will find you a better place than this to lie down and hide in. If I take one side of the way and you the other, to avoid observation, you will not 'hook it,' I know very well, if you make me a promise."

"I won't not unless I wos to see *him* a-coming, sir."

"Very well. I take your word. Half the town is getting up by this time, and the whole town will be broad awake in another hour. Come along. Good-day again, my good woman."

So Jo was taken to a clean little room, and bathed, and had clean clothes, and good food, and kind people about him once more, but he was too ill now, far too ill, for anything to do him any good.

"Let me lie here quiet," said poor Jo, "and be so kind anyone as is passin' nigh where I used to sweep, as to say to Mr. Snagsby as Jo, wot he knew once, is a-moving on."

One day the young doctor was sitting by him, when suddenly Jo made a strong effort to get out of bed.

"Well, Jo! what is the matter? Don't be frightened."

"I thought," says Jo, who has started and is looking round, "I thought I was in Tom-all-Alones again. An't there nobody here but you, Mr. Woodcot?"

"Nobody."

"And I an't took back to Tom-all-Alones. Am I, sir?"

"No." Jo closes his eyes, muttering, "I'm wery thankful."

After watching him closely a little while, Allan puts his mouth very near his ear, and says to him in a low, distinct voice:

"Jo! Did you ever know a prayer?"

"Never know'd nothink, sir."

"Not so much as one short prayer?"

"No, sir. Nothink at all. Mr. Chadbands he wos a-prayin' wunst at

Mr. Snagsby's and I heerd him, but he sounded as if he wos a-speakin' to his-self, and not to me. He prayed a lot, but *I* couldn't make out nothink on it. Different times there wos other genlmen come down Tom-all-Alones a-prayin', but they all mostly sed as the t'other wuns prayed wrong, and all mostly sounded to be a-talking to their-selves, or a passing blame on the t'others, and not a-talkin' to us. *We* never know'd nothink. *I* never know'd what it wos all about."

It takes him a long time to say this; and few but an experienced and attentive listener could hear, or, hearing, understand him. After a short relapse into sleep or stupor, he makes, of a sudden, a strong effort to get out of bed.

"Stay, Jo, stay! What now?"

"It's time for me to go to that there berryin ground, sir," he returns with a wild look.

"Lie down, and tell me. What burying-ground, Jo?"

"Where they laid him as wos wery good to me: wery good to me indeed, he wos. It's time for me to go down to that there berryin ground, sir, and ask to be put along with him. I wants to go there and be berried. He used fur to say to me, 'I am as poor as you to-day, Jo,' he ses. I wants to tell him that I am as poor as him now, and have come there to be laid along with him."

"By-and-by, Jo. By-and-by."

"Ah! P'r'aps they wouldn't do it if I wos to go myself. But will you promise to have me took there, sir, and laid along with him?"

"I will, indeed."

"Thank'ee, sir. Thank'ee, sir! They'll have to get the key of the gate afore they can take me in, for it's allus locked. And there's a step there, as I used fur to clean with my broom. It's turned wery dark, sir. Is there any light a-comin'?"

"It is coming fast, Jo."

Fast. The cart is shaken all to pieces, and the rugged road is very near its end.

"Jo, my poor fellow!"

"I hear you, sir, in the dark, but I'm a-gropin'—a-gropin'—let me catch hold of your hand."

"Jo, can you say what I say?"

"I'll say anythink as you say, sir, for I knows it's good."

"OUR FATHER."

"Our Father!—yes, that's wery good, sir?"

"WHICH ART IN HEAVEN."

"Art in Heaven—is the light a-comin', sir?"

"It is close at hand. HALLOWED BE THY NAME!"

"Hallowed be—Thy—name!"

The light is come upon the dark benighted way. Dead!

Dead, your Majesty. Dead, my lords and gentlemen. Dead, Right Reverends and Wrong Reverends of every order. Dead, men and women born with heavenly compassion in your hearts. And dying thus around us every day!

Little Nell.

LITTLE NELL.

THE house was one of those receptacles for old and curious things, which seem to crouch in odd corners of the town, and to hide their musty treasures from the public eye in jealousy and distrust. There were suits of mail standing like ghosts in armor, here and there; fantastic carvings brought from monkish cloisters; rusty weapons of various kinds; distorted figures in china, and wood, and iron, and ivory; tapestry, and strange furniture that might have been designed in dreams; and in the old, dark, murky rooms there lived alone together an old man and a child—his grandchild, Little Nell. Solitary and monotonous as was her life, the innocent and cheerful spirit of the child found happiness in all things, and, through the dim rooms of the old curiosity shop Little Nell went singing, moving with gay and lightsome step.

But gradually over the old man, to whom she was so tenderly attached, there stole a sad change. He became thoughtful, dejected, and wretched. He had no sleep or rest but that which he took by day in his easy-chair; for every night, and all night long, he was away from home. To the child it seemed that her grandfather's love for her increased, even with the hidden grief by which she saw him struck down. And to see him sorrowful, and not to know the cause of his sorrow; to see him growing pale and weak under his agony of mind, so weighed upon her gentle spirit that at times she felt as though her heart must break.

At last the time came when the old man's feeble frame could bear up no longer against his hidden care. A raging fever seized him, and, as he lay delirious or insensible through many weeks, Nell learned that the house which sheltered them was theirs no longer; that in the future they would be very poor; that they would scarcely have bread to eat.

At length the old man began to mend, but his mind was weakened.

He would sit for hours together, with Nell's small hand in his, playing with the fingers, and sometimes stopping to smooth her hair or kiss her brow; and when he saw that tears were glistening in her eyes he would look amazed. As the time drew near when they must leave the house, he made no reference to the necessity of finding other shelter. An indistinct idea he had that the child was desolate and in need of help; though he seemed unable to contemplate their real position more distinctly. But a change came upon him one evening, as he and Nell sat silently together.

"Let us speak softly, Nell," he said. "Hush! for if they knew our purpose they would say that I was mad, and take thee from me. We will not stop here another day. We will travel afoot through the fields and woods, and trust ourselves to God in the places where He dwells. To-morrow morning, dear, we'll turn our faces from this scene of sorrow, and be as free and happy as the birds."

The child's heart beat high with hope and confidence. She had no thought of hunger, or cold, or thirst, or suffering. To her it seemed that they might beg their way from door to door in happiness, so that they were together.

When the day began to glimmer they stole out of the house, and, passing into the street, stood still.

"Which way?" asked the child.

The old man looked irresolutely and helplessly at her, and shook his head. It was plain that she was thenceforth his guide and leader. The child felt it, but had no doubts or misgivings, and, putting her hand in

THE DEPARTURE OF LITTLE NELL AND HER GRANDFATHER.

his, led him gently away. Forth from the city, while it yet slumbered. went the two poor adventurers, wandering they knew not whither.

They passed through the long, deserted streets, in the glad light of early morning, until these streets dwindled away, and the open country was about them. They walked all day, and slept that night at a small cottage where beds were let to travelers. The sun was setting on the second day of their journey, and they were jaded and worn out with walking, when, following a path which led through a churchyard to the town where they were to spend the night, they fell in with two traveling showmen, exhibitors of a Punch and Judy show. They raised their eyes when the old man and his young companion were close upon them. One of them, the actual exhibitor, no doubt, was a little, merry-faced man with a twinkling eye and a red nose, who seemed to have unconsciously imbibed something of his hero's character. The other—that was he who took the money—had rather a careful and cautious look, which was perhaps inseparable from his occupation also.

The merry man was the first to greet the strangers with a nod; and following the old man's eyes, he observed that perhaps that was the first time he had ever seen a Punch off the stage. (Punch, it may be remarked, seemed to be pointing with the tip of his cap to a most flourishing epitaph, and to be chuckling over it with all his heart.)

"Why do you come here to do this?" said the old man, sitting down beside them, and looking at the figures with extreme delight.

"Why, you see," rejoined the little man, "we're putting up for tonight at the public house yonder, and it wouldn't do to let 'em see the present company undergoing repair."

"No!" cried the old man, making signs to Nell to listen, "why not, eh? why not?"

"Because it would destroy all the delusion and take away all the interest, wouldn't it?" replied the little man. "Would you care a ha'penny for the Lord Chancellor if you know'd him in private and without his wig?—certainly not."

"Good!" said the old man, venturing to touch one of the puppets, and drawing away his hand with a shrill laugh. "Are you going to show 'em to-night? are you?"

"That is the intention, governor," replied the other. "and unless I'm

CODLIN

much mistaken, Tommy Codlin is a-calculating at this minute what we've lost through your coming upon us.   Cheer up, Tommy, it can't be much."

The little man accompanied these latter words with a wink, expressive of the estimate he had formed of the travelers' pocketbook.

To this Mr. Codlin, who had a surly, grumbling manner, replied, as he twitched Punch off the tombstone and flung him into the box:

"I don't care if we haven't lost a farden, but you're too free.   If you stood in front of the curtain and see the public's faces as I do, you'd know human na-tur' better."

Turning over the figures in the box like one who knew and despised them, Mr. Codlin drew one forth and held it up for the inspection of his friend:

"Look here; here's all this Ju-dy's clothes falling to pieces again. You haven't got a needle and thread, I suppose?"

THE EXHIBITORS OF THE PUNCH AND JUDY SHOW.

The little man shook his head and scratched it ruefully, as he contemplated this severe indisposition of a principal performer.   Seeing that they were at a loss, the child said, timidly:

"I have a needle, sir, in my basket, and thread too.   Will you let me try to mend it for you!   I think I could do it neater than you could."

Even Mr. Codlin had nothing to urge against a proposal so seasonable. Nell, kneeling down beside the box, was soon busily engaged in her task, and accomplishing it to a miracle.

While she was thus engaged, the merry little man looked at her with an interest which did not appear to be diminished when he glanced at her helpless companion. When she had finished her work he thanked her, and inquired whither they were traveling.

"N—no farther to-night, I think," said the child, looking toward her grandfather.

"If you're wanting a place to stop at," the man remarked, "I should advise you to take up at the same house with us. That's it. The long, low, white house there. It's very cheap."

When they had been refreshed, the whole house hurried away into an empty stable where the show stood, and where, by the light of a few flaring candles stuck round a hoop which hung by a line from the ceiling, it was to be forthwith exhibited.

And now Mr. Thomas Codlin, after blowing away at the Pan's pipes, took his station on one side of the checked drapery which concealed the mover of the figures, and, putting his hands in his pockets, prepared to reply to all questions and remarks of Punch, and to make a dismal feint of being his most intimate private friend, of believing in him to the fullest and most unlimited extent, of knowing that he enjoyed day and night a merry and glorious existence in that temple, and that he was at all times and under every circumstance the same intelligent and joyful person that the spectators then beheld him.

The whole performance was applauded to the echo, and voluntary contributions were showered in with a liberality which testified yet more strongly to the general delight. Among the laughter none was more loud and frequent than the old man's. Nell's was unheard, for she, poor child, with her head drooping on his shoulder, had fallen asleep, and slept too soundly to be roused by any of his efforts to awaken her to a participation in his glee.

The supper was very good, but she was too tired to eat, and yet would not leave the old man until she had kissed him in his bed. He, happily insensible to every care and anxiety, sat listening with a vacant smile and admiring face to all that his new friends said; and it was not until they retired yawning to their room that he followed the child upstairs.

She had a little money, but it was very little, and when that was gone they must begin to beg. There was one piece of gold among it, and an emergency might come when its worth to them would be increased a

hundredfold. It would be best to hide this coin, and never produce it unless their case was absolutely desperate, and no other resource was left them.

Her resolution taken, she sewed the piece of gold into her dress, and going to bed with a lighter heart sunk into a deep slumber.

"And where are you going to-day?" said the little man the following morning, addressing himself to Nell.

"Indeed I hardly know—we have not determined yet," replied the child.

"We're going on to the races," said the little man. "If that's your way and you like to have us for company, let us travel together. If you prefer going alone, only say the word and you'll find that we shan't trouble you.'

"We'll go with you," said the old man. "Nell—with them, with them."

The child considered for a moment, and reflecting that she must shortly beg, and could scarcely hope to do so at a better place than where crowds of rich ladies and gentlemen were assembled together for purposes of enjoyment and festivity, determined to accompany these men so far. She therefore thanked the little man for his offer, and said, glancing timidly toward his friend, that they would if there was no objection to their accompanying them as far as the race-town.

And with these men they traveled forward on the following day.

They made two long days' journey with their new companions, passing through villages and towns, and meeting upon one occasion with two young people walking upon stilts, who were also going to the races.

And now they had come to the time when they must beg their bread. Soon after sunrise the second morning she stole out, and, rambling into some fields at a short distance, plucked a few wild roses and such humble flowers, purposing to make them into little nosegays and offer them to the ladies in the carriages when the company arrived. Her thoughts were not idle while she was thus employed; when she returned and was seated beside the old man, tying her flowers together, while the two men lay dozing in a corner, she plucked him by the sleeve, and, slightly glancing toward them, said, in a low voice:

"Grandfather, don't look at those I talk of, and don't seem as if I spoke of anything but what I am about. What was that you told me before we left the old house? That if they knew what we were going to do, they would say that you were mad, and part us?"

The old man turned to her with an aspect of wild terror; but she checked him by a look, and bidding him hold some flowers while she tied them up, and so bringing her lips closer to his ear, said:

"I know that was what you told me. You needn't speak, dear. I recollect it very well. It was not likely that I should forget it. Grandfather, these men I have heard suspect that we have secretly left our friends, and mean to carry us before some gentleman and have us taken care of and sent back. If you let your hand tremble so, we can never get away from them, but if you're only quiet now, we shall do so easily."

"How?" muttered the old man. "Dear Nell, how? They will shut me up in a stone-room, dark and cold, and chain me up to the wall, Nell —flog me with whips, and never let me see thee more!"

"You're trembling again," said the child. "Keep close to me all day. Never mind them, don't look at them, but me. I shall find a time when we can steal away. When I do, mind you come with me, and do not stop or speak a word. Hush! That's all."

"Halloo! what are you up to, my dear?" said Mr. Codlin, raising his head, and yawning.

"Making some nosegays," the child replied; "I am going to try and sell some, these three days of the races. Will you have one—as a present, I mean?"

Mr. Codlin would have risen to receive it, but the child hurried toward him and placed it in his hand, and he stuck it in his button-hole.

As the morning wore on, the tents at the race-course assumed a gayer and more brilliant appearance, and long lines of carriages came rolling softly on the turf. Black-eyed gypsy girls, hooded in showy handkerchiefs, sallied forth to tell fortunes, and pale, slender women with consumptive faces lingered upon the footsteps of ventriloquists and conjurers, and counted the sixpences with anxious eyes long before they were gained. As many of the children as could be kept within bounds were stowed away, with all the other signs of dirt and poverty, among the donkeys, carts, and horses; and as many as could not be thus disposed of ran in and out in all intricate spots, crept between people's legs and carriage wheels, and came forth unharmed from under horses' hoofs. The dancing-dogs, the stilts, the little lady and the tall man, and all the other attractions, with organs out of number and bands innumerable, emerged from the holes and corners in which they had passed the night, and flourished boldly in the sun.

Along the uncleared course, Short led his party, sounding the brazen trumpet and reveling in the voice of Punch; and at his heels went Thomas Codlin, bearing the show as usual, and keeping his eye on Nell and her grandfather, as they rather lingered in the rear. The child bore upon her arm the little basket with her flowers, and sometimes stopped, with timid and modest looks, to offer them at some gay carriage; but alas! there were many bolder beggars there, gypsies who promised husbands, and other adepts in their trade; and although some ladies smiled gently as they shook their heads,

THEY LAID DOWN AT NIGHT WITH NOTHING BETWEEN THEM AND THE SKY.

and others cried to the gentlemen beside them, "See what a pretty face!" they let the pretty face pass on, and never thought that it looked tired or hungry.

There was but one lady who seemed to understand the child, and she was one who sat alone in a handsome carriage, while two young men in dashing clothes, who had just dismounted from it, talked and laughed loudly at a little distance, appearing to forget her, quite. There were many ladies all around, but they turned their backs, or looked another way, or at the two young men (not unfavorably at *them*), and left her to herself. She motioned away a gypsy woman urgent to tell her fortune, saying that it was told already and had been for some years, but called the child toward her, and, taking her flowers, put money into her trembling hand, and bade her go home and keep at home.

Many a time they went up and down those long, long lines, seeing everything but the horses and the race; when the bell rung to clear the course, going back to rest among the carts and donkeys, and not coming out again until the heat was over. Many a time, too, was Punch displayed in the full zenith of his humor; but all this while the eye of Thomas Codlin was upon them, and to escape without notice was impracticable.

At length, late in the day, Mr. Codlin pitched the show in a convenient spot, and the spectators were soon in the very triumph of the scene.

If they were ever to get away unseen, that was the very moment. Short was plying the quarter-staves vigorously and knocking the characters in the fury of the combat against the sides of the show, the people were looking on with laughing faces, and Mr. Codlin had relaxed into a grim smile as his roving eye detected hands going into waistcoat pockets. If they were ever to get away unseen, that was the very moment. They seized it, and fled.

They made a path through booths and carriages and throngs of people, and never once stopped to look behind. The bell was ringing, and the course was cleared by the time they reached the ropes, but they dashed across it, insensible to the shouts and screeching that assailed them for breaking in upon its sanctity, and, creeping under the brow of the hill at a quick pace, made for the open fields.

That night they reached a little village in a woody hollow. The village schoolmaster, a good and gentle man, pitying their weariness, and attracted by the child's sweetness and modesty, gave them a lodging for the night; nor would he let them leave him until two days more had passed.

They journeyed on, when the time came that they must wander forth again, by pleasant country lanes; and as they passed, watching the birds that perched and twittered in the branches overhead, or listening to the songs that broke the happy silence, their hearts were tranquil and serene. But by-and-by they came to a long winding road which lengthened out far into the distance, and though they still kept on, it was at a much slower pace, for they were now very weary and fatigued.

The afternoon had worn away into a beautiful evening, when they arrived at a point where the road made a sharp turn and struck across a common. On the border of this common, and close to the hedge which divided it from the cultivated fields, a caravan was drawn up to rest; upon which, by reason of its situation, they came so suddenly that they could not have avoided it if they would.

It was not a shabby, dingy, dusty cart, but a smart little house upon wheels, with white dimity curtains festooning the windows, and window-shutters of green picked out with panels of a staring red, in which happily-contrasted colors the whole concern shone brilliant. Neither was it a poor caravan drawn by a single donkey or emaciated horse, for a pair of horses in pretty good condition were released from the shafts and grazing on the frouzy grass. Neither was it a gypsy cara-van, for at the open

"UPON ONE OCCASION THEY MET TWO YOUNG PEOPLE WALKING ON STILTS."

door (graced with a bright brass knocker) sat a Christian lady, stout and comfortable to look upon, who wore a large bonnet trembling with bows. And that it was not an unprovided or destitute caravan was clear from this lady's occupation, which was the very pleasant and refreshing one of taking tea. The tea-things, including a bottle of rather suspicious character and a cold knuckle of ham, were set forth upon a drum, covered with a white napkin; and there, as if at the most con-venient round-table in all the world, sat this roving lady, taking her tea and enjoying the prospect.

It happened at that moment that the lady of the caravan had her cup (which, that everything about her might be of a stout and comfortable kind, was a breakfast cup) to her lips, and that having her eyes lifted to the sky in her enjoyment of the full flavor of her tea, it happened that, being thus agreeably engaged, she did not see the travelers when they first came up. It was not until she was in the act of setting down the

MRS. JARLEY.

cup, and drawing a long breath after the exertion of causing its contents to disappear, that the lady of the caravan beheld an old man and a young child walking slowly by, and glancing at her proceedings with eyes of modest but hungry admiration.

"Hey!" cried the lady of the caravan, scooping the crumbs out of her lap and swallowing the same before wiping her lips. "Yes, to be sure —— Who won the Helter-Skelter Plate, child?"

"Won what, ma'am?" asked Nell.

"The Helter-Skelter Plate at the races, child—the plate that was run for on the second day."

"On the second day, ma'am?"

"Second day! Yes, second day," repeated the lady, with an air of impatience. "Can't you say who won the Helter-Skelter Plate when you're asked the question civilly?"

"I don't know, ma'am."

"Don't know!" repeated the lady of the caravan; "why, you were there. I saw you with my own eyes."

Nell was not a little alarm d to hear this, supposing that the lady might be intimately acquainted with the firm of Short and Codlin; but what followed tended to reassure her.

"And very sorry I was," said the lady ot the caravan, "to see you in company with a Punch—a low, practical, vulgar wretch, that people should scorn to look at."

"I was not there by choice," returned the child; "we didn't know our way, and the two men were very kind to us, and let us travel with them. Do you—do you know them, ma'am?"

"Know 'em, child?" cried the lady of the caravan, in a sort of shriek. "Know *them!* But you're young and inexperienced, and that's your excuse for asking sich a question. Do I look as if I know'd 'em? does the caravan look as if *it* know'd 'em?"

"No, ma'am, no," said the child, fearing she had committed some grievous fault. "I beg your pardon."

The lady of the caravan was in the act of gathering her tea equipage together preparatory to clearing the table, but noting the child's anxious manner, she hesitated and stopped. The child courtesied, and, giving her hand to the old man, had already got some fifty yards or so away, when the lady of the caravan called to her to return.

"Come nearer, nearer still," said she, beckoning to her to ascend the steps. "Are you hungry, child?"

"Not very, but we are tired, and it's—it *is* a long way——"

"Well, hungry or not, you had better have some tea," rejoined her new acquaintance. "I suppose you are agreeable to that, old gentleman?"

The grandfather humbly pulled off his hat and thanked her. The lady of the caravan then bade him come up the steps likewise, but the drum proving an inconvenient table for two, they descended again, and sat upon the grass, where she handed down to them the tea-tray, the bread and butter, and the knuckle of ham.

"Set 'em out near the hind wheels, child, that's the best place," said their friend, superintending the arrangements from above. "Now hand up the tea-pot for a little more hot water and a pinch of fresh tea, and then both of you eat and drink as much as you can, and don't spare anything; that's all I ask of you."

LITTLE NELL AND HER GRANDFATHER

The mistress of the caravan, saying the girl and her grandfather could not be very heavy, invited them to go along with them for a while, for which Nell thanked her with unaffected earnestness.

When they had traveled slowly forward for some short distance, Nell ventured to steal a look round the caravan and observe it more closely. One-half of it--that moiety in which the comfortable proprietress was then seated--was carpeted, and so partitioned off at the farther end as to accommodate a sleeping-place, constructed after the fashion of a berth on board ship, which was shaded, like the little windows, with fair white curtains, and looked comfortable enough, though by what kind of gymnastic exercise the lady of the caravan ever contrived to get into it was an unfathomable mystery. The other half served for a kitchen, and was fitted up with a stove whose small chimney passed through the roof.

The mistress sat looking at the child for a long time in silence, and then, getting up, brought out from a corner a large roll of canvas about a yard in width, which she laid upon the floor and spread open with her foot until it nearly reached from one end of the caravan to the other.

"There, child," she said, "read that."

Nell walked down it, and read aloud, in enormous black letters, the inscription, "JARLEY'S WAX-WORK."

"Read it again," said the lady, complacently.

"Jarley's Wax-work," repeated Nell.

"That's me," said the lady. "I am Mrs. Jarley."

Giving the child an encouraging look, the lady of the caravan unfolded another scroll, whereon was the inscription, "One hundred figures the full size of life;" and then another scroll, on which was written, "The only stupendous collection of real wax-work in the world;" and then several smaller scrolls, with such inscriptions as "Now exhibiting within"--"The genuine and only Jarley"--"Jarley's unrivaled collection"--"Jarley is the delight of the Nobility and Gentry"--"The Royal Family are the patrons of Jarley." When she had exhibited these leviathans of public announcement to the astonished child, she brought forth specimens of the lesser fry in the shape of handbills, some of which were couched in the form of parodies on popular melodies, as "Believe me if all Jarley's wax-work so rare"--"I saw thy show in youthful prime"--"Over the water to Jarley;" while, to consult all tastes, others were composed with a view to the lighter and more facetious spirits, as a parody on the favorite air of " If I had a donkey," beginning

> If I know'd a donkey wot wouldn't go
> To see MRS. JARLEY's wax-work show,
> Do you think I'd acknowledge him?
> Oh no, no!
>   Then run to Jarley's——

besides several compositions in prose, purporting to be dialogues between the Emperor of China and an oyster.

"I never saw any wax-work, ma'am," said Nell. "Is it funnier than Punch?"

"Funnier!" said Mrs. Jarley, in a shrill voice. "It is not funny at all."

"Oh!" said Nell, with all possible humility.

"It isn't funny at all," repeated Mrs. Jarley. "It's calm and—what's that word again—critical?—no—classical, that's it —it's calm and classical. No low beatings and knockings about, no jokings and squeakings like your precious Punches, but always the same, with a constantly unchanging air of coldness and gentility; and so like life that, if wax-work only spoke and walked about, you'd hardly know the difference. I won't go so far as

WITH A WILLOW WAND NELL POINTED OUT THE CHARACTERS IN MRS. JARLEY'S WAX-WORK.

to say that, as it is, I've seen wax-work quite like life, but I've certainly seen some life that was exactly like wax-work."

This conference at length concluded, she beckoned Nell to sit down.

"And the old gentleman, too," said Mrs. Jarley; "for I want to have a word with him. Do you want a good situation for your grand-daughter, master? If you do, I can put her in the way of getting one. What do you say?"

"I can't leave her," answered the old man. "We can't separate. What would become of me without her?"

" If you're really disposed to employ yourself," said Mrs. Jarley, " there would be plenty for you to do in the way of helping to dust the figures, and take the checks, and so forth. What I want your grand-daughter for is to point 'em out to the company ; they would be soon learned, and she has a way with her that people wouldn't thing unpleasant, though she *does* come after me ; for I've been always accustomed to go round with visitors myself, which I should keep on doing now, only that my spirits make a little ease absolutely necessary. It's not a common offer, bear in mind," said the lady, rising into the tone and manner in which she was accustomed to address her audiences ; " it's Jarley's wax-work, re-member. The duty's very light and genteel, the company particularly select, the exhibition takes place in assembly-rooms, town-halls, large rooms at inns, or auction galleries. There is none of your open-air wagrancy at Jarley's, recollect ; there is no tarpaulin and sawdust at Jarley's, remember. Every expectation held out in the handbills is realized to the utmost, and the whole forms an effect of imposing bril-liancy hitherto unrivaled in this kingdom. Remember that the price of admission is only sixpence, and that this is an opportunity which may never occur again !

" We are very much obliged to you, ma'am " said Nell, " and thank-fully accept your offer."

" And you'll never be sorry for it," returned Mrs. Jarley. " I'm pretty sure of that. So as that's all settled, let us have a bit of supper."

Rumbling along with most unwonted noise, the caravan stopped at last at the place of exhibition, where Nell dismounted amidst an admir-ing group of children, who evidently supposed her to be an important item of the curiosities, and were fully impressed with the belief that her grandfather was a cunning device in wax. The chests were taken out of the van for the figures with all convenient dispatch, and taken in to be unlocked by Mrs. Jarley, who, attended by George and the driver, disposed their contents (consisting of red festoons and other ornamental devices in upholstery work) to the best advantage in the decoration of the roo

When the festoons were all put up as tastily as they might be, the stupendous collection was uncovered, and there were displayed, on a raised platform some two feet from the floor, running round the room and parted from the rude public by a crimson rope, breast high, divers sprightly effigies of celebrated characters, singly and in groups, clad in

glittering dresses of various climes and times, and standing more or less unsteadily upon their legs, with their eyes very wide open, and their nostrils very much inflated, and the muscles of their legs and arms

NELL AND HER GRANDFATHER IN THE CHURCHYARD.

very strongly developed, and all their countenances expressing great surprise. All the gentlemen were very pigeon-breasted and very blue about the beards; and all the ladies were miraculous figures; and all the ladies and all the gentlemen were looking intensely nowhere, and staring with extraordinary earnestness at nothing.

When Nell had exhausted her first raptures at this glorious sight, Mrs. Jarley ordered the room to be cleared of all but herself and the child, and, sitting herself down in an arm-chair in the centre, formally invested Nell with a willow wand, long used by herself for pointing out the characters, and was at great pains to instruct her in her duty.

"That," said Mrs. Jarley, in her exhibition tone, as Nell touched a figure at the beginning of the platform, "is an unfortunate maid of honor in the time of Queen Elizabeth, who died from pricking her finger in consequence of working upon a Sunday. Observe the blood which is trickling from her finger; also the gold-eyed needle of the period, with which she is at work."

All this Nell repeated twice or thrice—pointing to the finger and the needle at the right times; and then passed on to the next.

"That, ladies and gentlemen," said Mrs. Jarley, "is Jasper Packlemerton, of atrocious memory, who courted and married fourteen wives, and destroyed them all, by tickling the soles of their feet when they were sleeping in the consciousness of innocence and virtue. On being brought to the scaffold and asked if he was sorry for what he had done, he replied yes, he was sorry for having let 'em off so easy, and hoped all Christian husbands would pardon him the offense. Let this be a warning to all young ladies to be particular in the character of the gentlemen of their choice. Observe that his fingers are curled as if in the act of tickling, and that his face is represented with a wink, as he appeared when committing his barbarous murders."

When Nell knew all about Mr. Packlemerton, and could say it without faltering, Mrs. Jarley passed on to the fat man, and then to the thin man, the tall man, the short man, the old lady who died of dancing at a hundred and thirty-two, the wild boy of the woods, the woman who poisoned fourteen families with pickled walnuts, and other historical characters and interesting but misguided individuals. And so well did Nell profit by her instructions, and so apt was she to remember them, that by the time they had been shut up together for a couple of hours, she was in full possession of the history of the whole establishment, and perfectly competent to the enlightenment of visitors.

LITTLE NELL.

For some time her life and the life of the poor vacant old man passed quietly and happily.

But heavier sorrow was yet to come. One night, a holiday night for them, Nell and her grandfather went out to walk. A terrible thunderstorm coming on, they were forced to take refuge in a small public house; and here some sinister and ill-favored men were playing cards. The old man watched them with increasing interest and excitement, until his whole appearance underwent a complete change. His face was flushed and eager, his teeth set. With a hand that trembled violently he seized Nell's little purse, and in spite of her entreaties joined in the game, gambling with such a savage thirst for gain that the distressed and frightened child could almost better have borne to see him dead. The night was far advanced before the play came to an end, and they were forced to remain where they were until the morning. And in the night the child was wakened from her troubled sleep to find a figure in the room—a figure busying its hands about her garments, while its face was turned to her, listening and looking lest she should awake. It was her grandfather himself, his white face pinched and sharpened by the greediness which made his eyes unnaturally bright, counting the money of which his hands were robbing her.

Evening after evening, after that night, the old man would steal away, not to return until the night was far spent, demanding, wildly, money. And at last there came an hour when the child overheard him, tempted beyond his feeble powers of resistance, undertake to find more money to feed the desperate passion which had laid its hold upon his weakness by robbing Mrs. Jarley.

That night the child took her grandfather by the hand and led him forth. Through the strait streets and narrow outskirts of the town their trembling feet passed quickly; the child sustained by one idea—that they were flying from disgrace and crime, and that her grandfather's preservation must depend solely upon her firmness unaided by one word of advice or any helping hand; the old man following her as though she had been an angel messenger sent to lead him where she would.

The hardest part of all their wanderings was now before them. They slept in the open air that night, and on the following morning some men offered to take them a long distance on their barge. These men, though they were not unkindly, were very rugged, noisy fellows, and they drank and quarreled fearfully among themselves, to Nell's inexpressible terror. It rained, too, heavily, and she was wet and cold.   At last they reached the great city whither the barge was bound, and here they wandered up and down, being now penniless, and watched the faces of those who passed, to find among them a ray of encouragement or hope.   Ill in body, and sick to death at heart, the child needed her utmost firmness and resolution even to creep along.

They laid down that night, and the next night too, with nothing between them and the sky; a penny loaf was all they had had that day, and when the third morning came, it found the child much weaker, yet she made no complaint.   The great manufacturing city hemmed them in on every side, and seemed to shut out hope.

Faint and spiritless as they were, its streets were insupportable.   After humbly asking for relief at some few doors, and being repulsed, they agreed to make their way out of it as speedily as they could, and try if the inmates of any lone house beyond would have more pity on their exhausted state.

They were dragging themselves along through the last street, and the child felt that the time was close at hand when her enfeebled powers would bear no more.   There appeared before them, at this juncture, going in the same direction as themselves, a traveler on foot, who, with a portmanteau strapped to his back, leaned upon a stout stick as he walked, and read from a book which he held in his other hand.

It was not an easy matter to come up with him and beseech his aid, for he walked fast, and was a little distance in advance.   At length he stopped, to look more attentively at some passage in his book.   Animated with a ray of hope, the child shot on before her grandfather, and, going close to the stranger without rousing him by the sound of her footsteps, began, in a few faint words, to implore his help.

He turned his head.   The child clapped her hands together, uttered a wild shriek, and fell senseless at his feet.

It was the poor schoolmaster.   No other than the poor schoolmaster. Scarcely less moved and surprised by the sight of the child than she had been on recognizing him, he stood, for a moment, silent, without even the presence of mind to raise her from the ground.

But, quickly recovering his self-possession, he threw down his stick and book, and, dropping on one knee beside her, endeavored, by such simple means as occurred to him, to restore her to herself; while her grandfather, standing idly by, wrung his hands, and implored her, with many endearing expressions, to speak to him, were it only a word.

"She appears to be quite exhausted," said the schoolmaster, glancing upward into his face. "You have taxed her powers too far, friend."

"She is perishing of want," rejoined the old man. "I never thought how weak and ill she was till now."

"SHE WOULD STEAL INTO THE CHURCH AND SIT UPON THE TOMBS."

Casting a look upon him, half-reproachful and half-compassionate, the schoolmaster took the child in his arms, and, bidding the old man gather up her little basket and follow him directly, bore her away at his utmost speed.

There was a small inn within sight, to which, it would seem, he had been directing his steps when so unexpectedly overtaken. Toward this place he hurried with his unconscious burden, and rushing into the kitchen, and calling upon the company there assembled to make way for God's sake, deposited it on a chair before the fire.

The company, who rose in confusion on the schoolmaster's entrance, did as people usually do under such circumstances. Everybody called for his or her favorite remedy, which nobody brought; each cried for more air, at the same time carefully excluding what air there was, by closing round the object of sympathy; and all wondered why somebody else didn't do what it never appeared to occur to them might be done by themselves.

The landlady, however, who possessed more readiness and activity than any of them, and who had withal a quicker perception of the merits of the case, soon came running in, with a little hot brandy-and-water, followed by her servant-girl, carrying vinegar, hartshorn, smelling-salts, and such other restoratives; which, being duly administered, recovered the child so far as to enable her to thank them in a faint voice, and to extend her hand to the poor schoolmaster, who stood, with an anxious face, hard by. Without suffering her to speak another word, or so much as to stir a finger any more, the women straightway carried her off to bed; and, having covered her up warm, bathed her cold feet, and wrapped them in flannel, they dispatched a messenger for the doctor.

The doctor, who was a red-nosed gentleman with a great bunch of seals dangling below a waistcoat of ribbed black satin, arrived with all speed, and taking his seat by the bedside of poor Nell, drew out his watch, and felt her pulse. Then he looked at her tongue, then he felt her pulse again, and while he did so, he eyed the half-emptied wine-glass as if in profound abstraction.

"I should give her," said the doctor at length, "a teaspoonful, every now and then, of hot brandy-and-water."

"Why, that's exactly what we've done, sir!" said the delighted landlady.

"I should also," observed the doctor, who had passed the foot-bath on the stairs, "I should also," said the doctor, in the voice of an oracle, "put her feet in hot water and wrap them up in flannel. I should likewise," said the doctor, with increased solemnity, "give her something light for supper—the wing of a roasted fowl now——"

"Why, goodness gracious me, sir, it's cooking at the kitchen fire this instant!" cried the landlady. And so indeed it was, for the school-master had ordered it to be put down, and it was getting on so well that the doctor might have smelled it if he had tried; perhaps he did.

"You may then," said the doctor, rising gravely, "give her a glass of hot mulled port-wine, if she likes wine——"

"And a toast, sir?" suggested the landlady.

"Ay," said the doctor, in the tone of a man who makes a dignified concession. "And a toast—of bread. But be very particular to make it of bread, if you please, ma'am."

With which parting injunction, slowly and portentously delivered, the doctor departed, leaving the whole house in admiration of that wisdom which tallied so closely with their own. Everybody said he was a very shrewd doctor indeed, and knew perfectly what people's constitutions were; which there appears some reason to suppose he did.

While her supper was preparing, the child fell into a refreshing sleep, from which they were obliged to rouse her when it was ready. As she evinced extraordinary uneasiness on learning that her grandfather was below stairs, and as she was greatly troubled at the thought of their being apart, he took his supper with her. Finding her still very restless on this head, they made him up a bed in an inner room, to which he presently retired. The key of this chamber happened by good-fortune to be on that side of the door which was in Nell's room; she turned it on him when the landlady had withdrawn, and crept to bed again with a thankful heart.

The schoolmaster sat for a long time smoking his pipe by the kitchen fire, which was now deserted, thinking, with a very happy face, on the fortunate chance which had brought him so opportunely to the child's assistance.

The schoolmaster, as it appeared, was on his way to a new home. And when the child had recovered somewhat from her exhaustion, it was arranged that she and her grandfather should accompany him to the village whither he was bound, and that he should endeavor to find them some humble occupation by which they could subsist.

LiTTLE NELL.

It was a secluded village, lying among the quiet country scenes Nell loved. And here, her grandfather being tranquil and at rest, a great peace fell upon the spirit of the child. Often she would steal into the church, and, sitting down among the quiet figures carved upon the tombs,

would think of the sum- mer days and the
bright spring-time that wouid come; of the
rays of sun that would fall in, aslant those
sleeping forms; of the songs of birds, and
the sweet air that would steal in. What if the
spot awakened thoughts of death! It would
be no pain to sleep amid such sights and
sounds as these. For the time was drawing
nearer every day when Nell was to rest
indeed. She
never mur-
mured or com-
plained, but
faded like a
light upon a

DAY AFTER DAY THE OLD MAN WOULD SIT BESIDE HER GRAVE.

summer's evening and died. Day after day and all day long, the old man, broken-hearted and with no love or care for anything in life, would sit beside her grave with her straw hat and the little basket she had been used to carry, waiting till she should come to him again. At last they found him lying dead upon the stone. And in the church where they had often prayed and mused and lingered, hand in hand, the child and the old man slept together.

Little David Copperfield.

DAVID COPPERFIELD AND HIS MOTHER.

I, LITTLE DAVID COPPER-FIELD, lived with my mother in a pretty house in the village of Blunderstone in Suffolk. I had never known my father, who died before I could remember anything, and I had neither brothers nor sisters. I was fondly loved by my pretty young mother, and our kind, good servant, Peggotty, and was a very happy little fellow. We had very few friends, and the only relation my mother talked about was an aunt of my father's, a tall and rather terrible old lady, from all accounts, who had once been to see us when I was quite a tiny baby, and had been so angry to find I was not a little girl that she had left the house quite offended, and had never been heard of since. One visitor, a tall, dark gentleman, I did not like at all, and was rather inclined to be jealous that my mother should be so friendly with the stranger.

Peggotty and I were sitting one night by the parlor fire, alone. I had been reading to Peggotty about crocodiles. I was tired of reading, and dead sleepy; but having leave, as a high treat, to sit up until my mother came home from spending the evening at a neighbor's, I would rather have died upon my post (of course) than have gone to bed. I had reached that stage of sleepiness when Peggotty seemed to swell and grow immensely large. I propped my eyelids open with my two forefingers, and looked perseveringly at her as she sat at work; at the little house with a thatched roof, where the yard-measure lived; at her work-box with a sliding-lid, with a view of St. Paul's Cathedral (with a pink dome) painted on the top; at the brass thimble on her finger; at herself, whom I thought lovely. I felt so sleepy that I knew if I lost sight of anything, for a moment, I was gone.

"Peggotty," says I, suddenly, "were you ever married?"

"Lord, Master Davy!" replied Peggotty. "What's put marriage in your head?"

She answered with such a start that it quite awoke me. And then she stopped in her work and looked at me, with her needle drawn out to its thread's length.

"But *were* you ever married, Peggotty?" says I. "You are a very handsome woman, an't you?"

"Me handsome, Davy!" said Peggotty. "Lawk, no, my dear! But what put marriage in your head?"

"I don't know! You mustn't marry more than one person at a time, may you, Peggotty?"

"Certainly not," says Peggotty, with the promptest decision.

"But if you marry a person, and the person dies, why then you may marry another person, mayn't you, Peggotty?"

"You MAY," says Peggotty, "if you choose, my dear. That's a matter of opinion."

"But what is your opinion, Peggotty?" said I.

I asked her and looked curiously at her, because she looked so curiously at me.

"My opinion is," said Peggotty, taking her eyes from me, after a little indecision, and going on with her work, "that I never was married myself, Master Davy, and that I don't expect to be. That's all I know about the subject."

"You an't cross, I suppose, Peggotty, are you?" said I, after sitting quiet for a minute.

LITTLE DAVID COPPERFIELD.

I really thought she was, she had been so short with me; but I was quite mistaken; for she laid aside her work (which was a stocking of her own) and opening her arms wide, took my curly head within them, and gave it a good squeeze. I know it was a good squeeze, because, being very plump, whenever she made any little exertion after she was dressed, some of the buttons on the back of her gown flew off. And I recollect two bursting to the opposite side of the parlor, while she was hugging me.

One day Peggotty asked me if I would like to go with her on a visit to her brother at Yarmouth.

"Is your brother an agreeable man, Peggotty?" I inquired.

"Oh, what an agreeable man he is!" cried Peggotty. "Then there's the sea, and the boats and ships, and the fishermen, and the beach. And 'Am to play with."

Ham was her nephew. I was quite anxious to go when I heard of all these delights; but my mother, what would she do all alone? Peggotty told me my mother was going to pay a visit to some friends, and would be sure to let me go. So all was arranged, and we were to start the next day in the carrier's cart. I was so eager that I wanted to put my hat and coat on the night before! But when the time came to say good-by to my dear mamma, I cried a little, for I had never left her before. It was rather a slow way of traveling, and I was very tired and sleepy when I arrived at Yarmouth, and found Ham waiting to meet me. He was a great strong fellow, six feet high, and took me on his back and the box under his arm to carry both to the house. I was delighted to find that this house was made of a real big black boat, with a door and windows cut in the side, and an iron funnel sticking out of the roof for a chimney. Inside, it was very cozy and clean, and I had a tiny bedroom in the stern. I was very much pleased to find a dear little girl, about my own age, to play with, and after tea I said:

"Mr. Peggotty."

"Sir," says he.

"Did you give your son the name of Ham because you lived in a sort of ark?"

Mr. Peggotty seemed to think it a deep idea, but answered:

"No, sir. I never giv' him no name."

"Who gave him that name, then?" said I, putting question number two of the catechism to Mr. Peggotty.

"Why, sir, his father giv' it him," said Mr. Peggotty.

"I thought you were his father!"

"My brother Joe was *his* father," said Mr. Peggotty.

"Dead, Mr. Peggotty?" I hinted, after a respectful pause.

"Drowndead," said Mr. Peggotty.

I was very much surprised that Mr. Peggotty was not Ham's father, and began to wonder whether I was mistaken about his relationship to anybody else there. I was so curious to know that I made up my mind to have it out with Mr. Peggotty.

"Little Em'ly," I said, glancing at her. "She is your daughter, isn't she, Mr. Peggotty?"

"No, sir. My brother-in-law, Tom, was *her* father."

I couldn't help it. "—— Dead, Mr. Peggotty?" I hinted, after another respectful silence.

"Drowndead," said Mr. Peggotty.

I felt the difficulty of resuming the subject, but had not got to the bottom of it yet, and must get to the bottom somehow. So I said:

"Haven't you *any* children, Mr. Peggotty?"

"No, master," he answered, with a short laugh. "I'm a bacheldore."

"A bachelor!" I said, astonished. "Why, who's that, Mr. Peggotty?" Pointing to the person in the apron who was knitting.

"That's Missis Gummidge," said Mr. Peggotty.

"Gummidge, Mr. Peggotty?"

But at this point Peggotty—I mean my own Peggotty—made such impressive motions to me not to ask any more questions, that I could only sit and look at all the company, until it was time to go to bed.

Mrs. Gummidge lived with them too, and did the cooking and cleaning, for she was a poor widow and had no home of her own. I thought Mr. Peggotty was very good to take all these people to live with him, and I was quite right, for Mr. Peggotty was only a poor man himself and had to work hard to get a living.

Almost as soon as morning shone upon the oyster-shell frame of my mirror I was out of bed, and out with little Em'ly, picking up stones upon the beach.

DAVID COPPERFIELD

"You're quite a sailor, I suppose?" I said to Em'ly. I don't know that I supposed anything of the kind, but I felt it an act of gallantry to say something; and a shining sail close to us made such a pretty little image of itself, at the moment, in her bright eye, that it came into my head to say this.

"No," replied Em'ly, shaking her head, "I'm afraid of the sea."

"Afraid!" I said, with a becoming air of boldness, and looking very big at the mighty ocean. "*I* an't."

"Ah! but it's cruel," said Em'ly. "I have seen it very cruel to some of our men. I have seen it tear a boat as big as our house all to pieces."

"I hope it wasn't the boat that——"

"That father was drowned in?" said Em'ly. "No. Not that one, I never see that boat."

"Nor him?" I asked her.

Little Em'ly shook her head. "Not to remember!"

Here was a coincidence! I immediately went into an explanation how I had never seen my own father; and how my mother and I had always lived by ourselves in the happiest state imaginable, and lived so then, and always meant to live so; and how my father's grave was in the churchyard near our house, and shaded by a tree, beneath the boughs of which I had walked and heard the birds sing many a pleasant morning. But there were some differences between Em'ly's orphanhood and mine, it appeared. She had lost her mother before her father, and where her father's grave was no one knew, except that it was somewhere in the depths of the sea.

"Besides," said Em'ly, as she looked about for shells and pebbles, "your father was a gentleman and your mother is a lady; and my father was a fisherman and my mother was a fisherman's daughter, and my Uncle Dan is a fisherman."

"Dan is Mr. Peggotty, is he?" said I.

"Uncle Dan—yonder," answered Em'ly, nodding at the boat-house.

"Yes. I mean him. He must be very good, I should think."

"Good?" said Em'ly. "If I was ever to be a lady, I'd give him a sky-blue coat with diamond buttons, nankeen trousers, a red velvet waistcoat, a cocked hat, a large gold watch, a silver pipe, and a box of money."

LITTLE DAVID COPPERFIELD.

I said I had no doubt that Mr. Peggotty well deserved these treasures.

Little Em'ly had stopped and looked up at the sky in her enumeration of these articles, as if they were a glorious vision. We went on again, picking up shells and pebbles.

"You would like to be a lady?" I said.

Em'ly looked at me, and laughed and nodded **"yes."**

"I should like it very much. We would all be gentlefolks together, then. Me, and uncle, and Ham, and Mrs. Gummidge. We wouldn't mind then, when there come stormy weather. Not for our own sakes, I mean. We would for the poor fishermen's, to be sure, and we'd help 'em with money when they come to any hurt."

I was quite sorry to leave these kind people and my dear little companion, but still I was glad to think I should get back to my own dear mamma. When I reached home, however, I found a great change. My mother was married to the dark man I did not like, whose name was Mr. Murdstone, and he was a stern, hard man, who had no love for me, and did not allow my mother to pet and indulge me as she had done before. Mr. Murdstone's sister came to live with us, and as she was even more difficult to please than her brother, and disliked boys, my life was no longer a happy one. I tried to be good and obedient, for I knew it made my mother very unhappy to see me punished and found fault with. I had always had lessons with my mother, and as she was patient and gentle, I had enjoyed learning to read, but now I had a great many very hard lessons to do, and was so frightened and shy when Mr. and Miss Murdstone were in the room, that I did not get on at all well, and was continually in disgrace.

Let me remember how it used to be, and bring one morning back again.

I come into the second-best parlor after breakfast, with my books, and an exercise-book and a slate. My mother is ready for me at her writing-desk, but not half so ready as Mr. Murdstone in his easy-chair by the window (though he pretends to be reading a book), or as Miss Murdstone, sitting near my mother stringing steel beads. The very sight of these two has such an influence over me that I begin to feel the words I have been at infinite pains to get into my head all sliding away, and going I don't know where. I wonder where they *do* go, by-the-by?

I hand the first book to my mother. Perhaps it is a grammar, perhaps a history, or geography. I take a last drowning look at the page as I give it into her hand, and start off aloud at a racing pace while I have got it fresh. I trip over a word. Mr. Murdstone looks up. I trip over another word. Miss Murdstone looks up. I redden, tumble over half a dozen words, and stop. I think my mother would show me the book if she dared, but she does not dare, and she says softly .

"Oh, Davy, Davy!"

"Now, Clara," says Mr. Murdstone, "be firm with the boy. Don't say, 'Oh, Davy, Davy!' That's childish. He knows his lesson, or he does not know it."

"He does *not* know it," Miss Murdstone interposes awfully.

"I am really afraid he does not," says my mother.

"Then you see, Clara," returns Miss Murdstone, "you should just give him the book back, and make him know it."

"Yes, certainly," says my mother; "that is what I intend to do, my dear Jane. Now, Davy, try once more, and don't be stupid."

I obey the first clause of the injunction by trying once more, but am not so successful with the second, for I am very stupid. I tumble down before I get to the old place, at a point where I was all right before, and stop to think. But I can't think about the lesson. I think of the number of yards of net in Miss Murdstone's cap, or of the price of Mr. Murdstone's dressing-gown, or any such ridiculous problem that I have no business with, and don't want to have anything at all to do with. Mr. Murdstone makes a movement of impatience which I have been expecting for a long time. Miss Murdstone does the same. My mother glances submissively at them, shuts the book, and lays it by as an arrear to be worked out when my other tasks are done.

There is a pile of these arrears very soon, and it swells like a rolling snowball. The bigger it gets, the more stupid *I* get. The case is so hopeless, and I feel that I am wallowing in such a bog of nonsense, that I give up all idea of getting out, and abandon myself to my fate. The despairing way in which my mother and I look at each other, as I blunder on, is truly melancholy. But the greatest effect in these miserable lessons is when my mother (thinking nobody is observing her) tries to give me the cue by the motion of her lips. At that instant, Miss Murdstone, who has been lying in wait for nothing else all along, says in a deep warning voice:

"Clara!"

My mother starts, colors, and smiles faintly. Mr. Murdstone comes out of his chair, takes the book, throws it at me, or boxes my ears with it, and turns me out of the room by the shoulders.

My only pleasure was to go up into a little room at the top of the house where I had found a number of books that had belonged to my own father, and I would sit and read Robinson Crusoe, and many tales of travels and adventures, and I imagined myself to be sometimes one and sometimes another hero, and went about for days with the centre-piece out of an old set of boot-trees, pretending to be a captain in the British Royal Navy.

One morning when I went into the parlor with my books, I found my mother looking anxious, Miss Murdstone looking firm, and Mr. Murdstone binding something round the bottom of a cane—a lithe and limber cane, which he left off binding when I came in, and poised and switched in the air.

"I tell you, Clara," said Mr. Murdstone, "I have often been flogged myself."

"To be sure; of course," said Miss Murdstone.

"Certainly, my dear Jane," faltered my mother, meekly. "But—but do you think it did Edward good?"

"Do you think it did Edward harm, Clara?" asked Mr. Murdstone, gravely.

"That's the point!" said his sister.

To this my mother returned, "Certainly, my dear Jane," and said no more.

I felt apprehensive that I was personally interested in this dialogue, and sought Mr. Murdstone's eye as it lighted on mine.

"Now, David," he said—and I saw that cast again, as he said it—"you must be far more careful to-day than usual." He gave the cane another poise and another switch; and having finished his preparation of it, laid it down beside him, with an expressive look, and took up his book.

This was a good freshener to my presence of mind, as a beginning. I felt the words of my lessons slipping off, not one by one, or line by line, but by the entire page. I tried to lay hold of them; but they seemed, if I may so express it, to have put skates on, and to skim away from me with a smoothness there was no checking.

We began badly, and went on worse. I had come in with an idea of distinguishing myself rather, conceiving that I was very well prepared; but it turned out to be quite a mistake. Book after book was added to the heap of failures, Miss Murdstone being firmly watchful of us all the time. And when we came at last to the five thousand cheeses (canes he made it that day, I remember), my mother burst out crying.

"Clara!" said Miss Murdstone, in her warning voice.

"I am not quite well, my dear Jane, I think," said my mother.

I saw him wink, solemnly, at his sister, as he rose and said, taking up the cane:

"Why, Jane, we can hardly expect Clara to bear, with perfect firmness, the worry and torment that David has occasioned her to-day. Clara is greatly strengthened and improved, but we can hardly expect so much from her. David, you and I will go upstairs, boy."

As he took me out at the door, my mother ran towards us. Miss Murdstone said, "Clara! are you a perfect fool?" and interfered. I saw my mother stop her ears then, and I heard her crying.

He walked me up to my room slowly and gravely—I am certain he had a delight in that formal parade of executing justice—and when we got there, suddenly twisted my head under his arm.

"Mr. Murdstone! Sir!" I cried to him. "Don't! Pray don't beat me! I have tried to learn, sir, but I can't learn while you and Miss Murdstone are by. I can't indeed!"

"Can't you, indeed, David?" he said. "We'll try that."

He had my head as in a vise, but I twined round him somehow, and stopped him for a moment, entreating him not to beat me. It was only for a moment that I stopped him, for he cut me heavily an instant afterwards, and in the same instant I caught the hand with which he held me in my mouth, between my teeth, and bit it through. It sets my teeth on edge to think of it.

He beat me then, as if he would have beaten me to death. Above all the noise we made, I heard them running up the stairs, and crying out

LITTLE DAVID COPPERFIELD.

—I heard my mother crying out—and Peggotty. Then he was gone; and the door was locked outside; and I was lying, fevered and hot, and torn, and sore, and raging in my puny way, upon the floor.

How well I recollect, when I became quiet, what an unnatural stillness seemed to reign through the whole house! How well I remember, when my smart and passion began to cool, how wicked I began to feel!

I sat listening for a long while, but there was not a sound. I crawled up from the floor, and saw my face in the glass, so swollen, red, and ugly that it almost frightened me. My stripes were sore and stiff, and made me cry afresh, when I moved; but they were nothing to the guilt I felt. It lay heavier on my breast than if I had been a most atrocious criminal, I dare say.

It had begun to grow dark, and I had shut the window (I had been lying, for the most part, with my head upon the sill, by turns crying, dozing, and looking listlessly out), when the key was turned, and Miss Murdstone came in with some bread and meat and milk. These she put down upon the table without a word, glaring at me the while with exemplary firmness, and then retired, locking the door after her.

I never shall forget the waking, next morning; the being cheerful and fresh for the first moment, and then the being weighed down by the stale and dismal oppression of remembrance. Miss Murdstone reappeared before I was out of bed; told me, in so many words, that I was free to walk in the garden for half an hour and no longer; and retired, leaving the door open, that I might avail myself of that permission.

I did so, and did so every morning of my imprisonment, which lasted five days. If I could have seen my mother alone, I should have gone down on my knees to her and besought her forgiveness; but I saw no one, Miss Murdstone excepted, during the whole time.

The length of those five days I can convey no idea of to anyone. They occupy the place of years in my remembrance.

On the last night of my restraint, I was awakened by hearing my own name spoken in a whisper. I started up in bed, and, putting out my arms in the dark, said:

"Is that you, Peggotty?"

There was no immediate answer, but presently I heard my name again, in a tone so very mysterious and awful, that I think I should have gone into a fit, if it had not occurred to me that it must have come through the keyhole.

I groped my way to the door, and, putting my own lips to the keyhole, whispered :

"Is that you, Peggotty, dear?"

"Yes, my own precious Davy," she replied. "Be as soft as a mouse, or the cat'll hear us."

I understood this to mean Miss Murdstone, and was sensible of the urgency of the case; her room being close by.

"How's mamma, dear Peggotty? Is she very angry with me?"

I could hear Peggotty crying softly on her side of the keyhole, as I was doing on mine, before she answered. "No. Not very."

"What is going to be done with me, Peggotty, dear? Do you know?"

"School. Near London," was Peggotty's answer. I was obliged to get her to repeat it, for she spoke it the first time quite down my throat in consequence of my having forgotten to take my mouth away from the keyhole and put my ear there; and, though her words tickled me a good deal, I didn't hear them.

"When, Peggotty?"

"To-morrow."

"Is that the reason why Miss Murdstone took the clothes out of my drawers?" which she had done, though I have forgotten to mention it.

"Yes," said Peggotty. "Box."

"Shan't I see mamma?"

"Yes," said Peggotty. "Morning."

Then Peggotty fitted her mouth close to the keyhole, and delivered these words through it with as much feeling and earnestness as a keyhole has ever been the medium of communicating, I will venture to assert, shooting in each broken little sentence in a convulsive little burst of its own.

"Davy, dear. If I ain't been azackly as intimate with you. Lately, as I used to be. It ain't because I don't love you. Just as well and more, my pretty poppet. It's because I thought it better for you. And for someone else besides. Davy, my darling, are you listening? Can you hear?"

"Ye—ye—ye—yes, Peggotty!" I sobbed.

LITTLE DAVID COPPERFIELD.

"My own!" said Peggotty, with infinite compassion. "What I want to say, is. That you must never forget me. For I'll never forget you. And I'll take as much care of your mamma, Davy. As I ever took of you. And I won't leave her. The day may come when she'll be glad to lay her poor head. On her stupid, cross old Peggotty's arm again. And I'll write to you, my dear. Though I ain't no scholar. And I'll—I'll—" Peggotty fell to kissing the keyhole, as she couldn't kiss me.

"Thank you, dear Peggotty!" said I. "Oh, thank you! Thank you! Will you promise me one thing, Peggotty? Will you write and tell Mr. Peggotty and little Em'ly and Mrs. Gummidge and Ham that I am not so bad as they might suppose, and that I sent 'em all my love—especially to little Em'ly? Will you, if you please, Peggotty?"

The kind soul promised, and we both of us kissed the keyhole with the greatest affection—I patted it with my hand, I recollect, as if it had been her honest face—and parted.

In the morning Miss Murdstone appeared as usual, and told me I was going to school; which was not altogether such news to me as she supposed. She also informed me that when I was dressed, I was to come downstairs into the parlor and have my breakfast. There I found my mother, very pale and with red eyes: into whose arms I ran, and begged her pardon from my suffering soul.

"Oh, Davy!" she said. "That you could hurt anyone I love! Try to be better, pray to be better! I forgive you; but I am so grieved, Davy, that you should have such bad passions in your heart."

Miss Murdstone was good enough to take me out to the cart, and to say on the way that she hoped I would repent, before I came to a bad end; and then I got into the cart, and the lazy horse walked off with it.

We might have gone about half a mile, and my pocket handkerchief was quite wet through, when the carrier stopped short.

Looking out to ascertain for what, I saw, to my amazement, Peggotty burst from a hedge and climb into the cart. She took me in both her arms and squeezed me until the pressure on my nose was extremely painful, though I never thought of that till afterwards, when I found it very tender. Not a single word did Peggotty speak. Releasing one of her arms, she put it down in her pocket to the elbow, and brought out some paper-bags of cakes, which she crammed into my pockets, and a purse which she put into my hand, but not one word did she say. After another and a final squeeze with both arms, she got down from the cart and ran away; and my belief is, and has always been, without a solitary button on her gown. I picked up one, of several that was rolling about, and treasured it as a keepsake for a long time.

The carrier looked at me, as if to enquire if she were coming back. I shook my head, and said I thought not. "Then come up!" said the carrier to the lazy horse, who came up accordingly.

Having by this time cried as much as I possibly could, I began to think it was of no use crying any more, especially as neither Roderick Random nor that captain in the Royal British Navy had ever cried, that I could remember, in trying situations. The carrier seeing me in this resolution, proposed that my pocket handkerchief should be spread upon the horse's back to dry. I thanked him and assented; and particularly small it looked under those circumstances.

I had now leisure to examine the purse. It was a stiff leather purse, with a snap, and had three bright shillings in it, which Peggotty had evidently polished up with whitening, for my greater delight. But its precious contents were two half-crowns folded together in a bit of paper, on which was written, in my mother's hand, "For Davy. With my love." I was so overcome by this, that I asked the carrier to be so good as reach me my pocket handkerchief again, but he said he thought I had better do without it; and I thought I really had, so I wiped my eyes on my sleeve and stopped myself.

For good, too; though, in consequence of my previous emotions, I was still occasionally seized with a stormy sob. After we had jogged on for some little time, I asked the carrier if he was going all the way.

"All the way where?" inquired the carrier.

"There," I said.

"Where's there?" inquired the carrier.

"Near London," I said.

"Why, that horse," said the carrier, jerking the rein to point him out, "would be deader than pork afore he got over half the ground."

"Are you only going to Yarmouth then?" I asked.

"That's about it," said the carrier. "And there I shall take you to the stage-cutch, and the stage-cutch that'll take you to—wherever it is."

LITTLE DAVID COPPERFIELD.

I shared my cakes with the carrier, who asked if Peggotty made them, and told him yes, she did all our cooking. The carrier looked thoughtful, and then asked if I would send a message to Peggotty from him. I agreed, and the message was "Barkis is willing." While I was waiting for the coach at Yarmouth, I wrote to Peggotty.

"MY DEAR PEGGOTTY :—I have come here safe. Barkis is willing. My love to mamma. Yours affectionately.

"P. S.—He says he particularly wanted you to know *Barkis is willing.*"

At Yarmouth I found dinner was ordered for me, and felt very shy at having a table all to myself, and very much alarmed when the waiter told me he had seen a gentleman fall down dead after drinking some of their beer. I said I would have some water, and was quite grateful to the waiter for drinking the ale that had been ordered for me, for fear the people of the hotel should be offended. He also helped me to eat my dinner, and accepted one of my bright shillings.

After a long, tiring journey by the coach, for there were no trains in those days, I arrived in London and was taken to the school at Blackheath, by one of the masters, Mr. Mell.

I gazed upon the schoolroom into which he took me, as the most forlorn and desolate place I had ever seen. I see it now. A long room, with three long rows of desks, and six of forms, and bristling all round with pegs for hats and slates. Scraps of old copy-books and exercises litter the dirty floor.

Mr. Mell having left me while he took his irreparable boots upstairs, I went softly to the upper end of the room, observing all this as I crept along. Suddenly I came upon a pasteboard placard, beautifully written, which was lying on the desk, and bore these words—"*Take care of him. He bites.*"

I got upon the desk immediately, apprehensive of at least a great dog underneath. But, though I looked all round with anxious eyes, I could see nothing of him. I was still engaged in peering about when Mr. Mell came back, and asked me what I did up there.

"I beg your pardon, sir," says I, "if you please, I'm looking for the dog."

"Dog?" says he.   "What dog?"

"Isn't it a dog, sir?"

"Isn't what a dog?"

LITTLE DAVID COPPERFIELD AND BARKIS.

"That's to be taken care of, sir; that bites."

"No, Copperfield," says he, gravely, "that's not a dog.   That's a boy. My instructions are, Copperfield, to put this placard on your back.   I am sorry to make such a beginning with you, but I must do it."

With that, he took me down, and tied the placard, which was neatly constructed for the purpose, on my shoulders like a knapsack; and wherever I went, afterwards, I had the consolation of carrying it.

LITTLE DAVID COPPERFIELD.

What I suffered from that placard, nobody can imagine. Whether it was possible for people to see me or not, I always fancied that somebody was reading it. It was no relief to turn round and find nobody; for wherever my back was, there I imagined somebody always to be.

There was an old door in this playground, on which the boys had a custom of carving their names. It was completely covered with such inscriptions. In my dread of the end of the vacation and their coming back, I could not read one boy's name, without inquiring in what tone and with what emphasis *he* would read, "Take care of him. He bites." There was one boy—a certain J. Steerforth—who cut his name very deep and very often, who, I conceived, would read it in a rather strong voice, and afterwards pull my hair. There was another boy, one Tommy Traddles, who I dreaded would make game of it, and pretend to be dreadfully frightened of me. There was a third, George Demple, who I fancied would sing it. I have looked, a little shrinking creature, at that door, until the owners of all the names—there were five-and-forty of them in the school then, Mr. Mell said—seemed to send me to Coventry by general acclamation, and to cry out, each in his own way, "Take care of him. He bites!"

Tommy Traddles was the first boy who returned. He introduced himself by informing me that I should find his name on the right-hand corner of the gate, over the top bolt; upon that I said, "Traddles?" to which he replied, "The same," and then he asked me for a full account of myself and family.

It was a happy circumstance for me that Traddles came back first. He enjoyed my placard so much that he saved me from the embarrassment of either disclosure or concealment, by presenting me to every other boy who came back, great or small, immediately on his arrival, in this form of introduction, "Look here! Here's a game!" Happily, too, the greater part of the boys came back low-spirited, and were not so boisterous at my expense as I had expected. Some of them certainly did dance about me like wild Indians, and the greater part could not resist the temptation of pretending that I was a dog, and patting and smoothing me lest I should bite, and saying, "Lie down, sir!" and calling me Towzer. This was naturally confusing, among so many strangers, and cost me some tears, but on the whole it was much better than I had anticipated.

I was not considered as being formally received into the school, however, until J. Steerforth arrived. Before this boy, who was reputed to be a great scholar, and was very good-looking, and at least half-a-dozen years my senior, I was carried as before a magistrate. He inquired, under a shed in the playground, into the particulars of my punishment, and was pleased to express his opinion that it was a "jolly shame;" for which I became bound to him ever afterwards.

"What money have you got, Copperfield?" he said, walking aside with me when he had disposed of my affair in these terms.

I told him seven shillings.

"You had better give it to me to take care of," he said. "At least, you can, if you like. You needn't if you don't like."

I hastened to comply with his friendly suggestion, and, opening Peggotty's purse, turned it upside down into his hand.

"Do you want to spend anything now?" he asked me.

"No, thank you," I replied.

"You can, if you like, you know," said Steerforth. "Say the word."

"No, thank you, sir," I repeated.

"Perhaps you'd like to spend a couple of shillings or so in a bottle of currant wine by-and-by, up in the bedroom?" said Steerforth. "You belong to my bedroom, I find."

It certainly had not occurred to me before, but I said, Yes, I should like that.

"Very good," said Steerforth. "You'll be glad to spend another shilling or so in almond cakes, I dare say?"

I said, Yes, I should like that, too.

"And another shilling or so in biscuits, and another in fruit, eh?" said Steerforth. "I say, young Copperfield, you're going it!"

I smiled because he smiled, but I was a little troubled in my mind, too.

"Well!" said Steerforth. "We must make it stretch as far as we can; that's all. I'll do the best in my power for you. I can go out when I like, and I'll smuggle the prog in." With these words he put the money in his pocket, and kindly told me not to make myself uneasy; he would take care it should be all right.

LITTLE DAVID COPPERFIELD.

He was as good as his word, if that were all right which I had a secret misgiving was nearly all wrong—for I feared it was a waste of my mother's two half-crowns—though I had preserved the piece of paper they were wrapped in; which was a precious saving. When we went upstairs to bed, he produced the whole seven shillings' worth, and laid it out on my bed in the moonlight, saying:

"There you are, young Copperfield, and a royal spread you've got!"

I couldn't think of doing the honors of the feast at my time of life, while he was by; my hand shook at the very thought of it. I begged him to do me the favor of presiding; and my request being seconded by the other boys who were in that room, he acceded to it, and sat upon my pillow, handing round the viands—with perfect fairness, I must say— and dispensing the currant wine in a little glass without a foot, which was his own property. As to me, I sat on his left hand, and the rest were grouped about us, on the nearest beds and on the floor.

How well I recollect our sitting there, talking in whispers; or their talking, and my respectfully listening, I ought rather to say; the moonlight falling a little way into the room, through the window, painting a pale window on the floor, and the greater part of us in shadow, except when Steerforth dipped a match into a phosphorus-box, when he wanted to look for anything on the board, and shed a blue glare over us that was gone directly! A certain mysterious feeling, consequent on the darkness, the secrecy of the revel, and the whisper in which everything was said, steals over me again, and I listen to all they tell me, with a vague feeling of solemnity and awe, which makes me glad they are all so near, and frightens me (though I feign to laugh) when Traddles pretends to see a ghost in the corner.

I heard all kinds of things about the school and all belonging to it. I heard that Mr. Creakle was the sternest and most severe of masters; that he laid about him, right and left, every day of his life, charging in among the boys like a trooper, and slashing away, unmercifully.

I heard that the man with the wooden leg, whose name was Tungay, was an obstinate barbarian who had formerly assisted in the hop business, but had come into the line with Mr. Creakle, in consequence, as was supposed among the boys, of his having broken his leg in Mr.

Creakle's service, and having done a deal of dishonest work for him, and knowing his secrets.

But the greatest wonder that I heard of Mr. Creakle was, there being one boy in the school on whom he never ventured to lay a hand, and that boy being J. Steerforth. Steerforth himself confirmed this when it was stated, and said that he should like to begin to see him do it. On being asked by a mild boy (not me) how he would proceed if he did begin to see him do it, he dipped a match into his phosphorus-box on purpose to shed a glare over his reply, and said he would commence with knocking him down with a blow on the forehead from the seven-and-six-penny ink-bottle that was always on the mantelpiece. We sat in the dark for some time, breathless.

I heard that Miss Creakle was regarded by the school in general as being in love with Steerforth; and I am sure, as I sat in the dark, think-ing of his nice voice, and his fine face, and his easy manner, and his curling hair, I thought it very likely. I heard that Mr. Mell was not a bad sort of fellow, but hadn't a sixpence to bless himself with: and that there was no doubt that old Mrs. Mell, his mother, was as poor as Job.

One day, Traddles (the most unfortunate boy in the world) breaks a window accidentally with a ball. I shudder at this moment with the tremendous sensation of seeing it done, and feeling that the ball has bounded on to Mr. Creakle's sacred head.

Poor Traddles! In a tight sky-blue suit that made his arms and legs like German sausages, or roly-poly puddings, he was the merriest and most miserable of all the boys. He was always being caned—I think he was caned every day that half-year, except one holiday Monday, when he was only rulered on both hands—and was always going to write to his uncle about it, and never did. After laying his head on the desk for a little while, he would cheer up somehow, begin to laugh again, and draw skele-tons all over his slate before his eyes were dry. I used at first to wonder what comfort Traddles found in drawing skeletons. But I believe he only did it because they were easy, and didn't want any features.

He was very honorable, Traddles was; and held it as a solemn duty in the boys to stand by one another. He suffered for this on several occasions; and particularly once, when Steerforth laughed in church, and the beadle thought it was Traddles, and took him out. I see him now, going **away in** custody, despised by the congregation. He never said who was the real offender, though he smarted for it next day, and was imprisoned so many hours that he came forth with a whole churchyard full of skeletons swarming all over his Latin Dictionary. But he had his reward. Steerforth said there was nothing of the sneak in Traddles, and we all felt that to be the highest praise. For my part, I could have gone through a great deal (though I was much less brave than Traddles, and nothing like so old) to have won such a recompense.

To see Steerforth walk to church before us, arm-in-arm with Miss Creakle, was one of the great sights of my life. I didn't think Miss Creakle equal to little Em'ly in point of beauty, and I didn't love her (I didn't dare); but I thought her a young lady of extraordinary attractions, and in point of gentility not to be surpassed. When Steerforth, in white trousers, carried her parasol for her, I felt proud to know him; and believed that she could not choose but adore him with all her heart. Mr. Sharp and Mr. Mell were both notable personages in my eyes; but Steerforth was to them what the sun was to two stars.

An accidental circumstance cemented the intimacy between Steerforth and me, in a manner that inspired me with great pride and satisfaction, though it sometimes led to inconvenience. It happened on one occasion, when he was doing me the honor of talking to me in the playground, that I hazarded the observation that something or somebody—I forget what now—was like something or somebody in Peregrine Pickle. He said nothing at the time; but when I was going to bed at night, asked me if I had got that book.

I told him no, and explained how it was that I had read it, and all those other books of which I had made mention.

"And do you recollect them?" Steerforth said.

Oh yes, I replied; I had a good memory, and I believed I recollected them very well.

"Then I tell you what, young Copperfield," said Steerforth, "you shall tell 'em to me. I can't get to sleep very early at night, and I generally wake rather early in the morning. We'll go over 'em one after another. We'll make some regular Arabian Nights of it."

I felt extremely flattered by this arrangement, **and we commenced carrying it into execution that very evening.**

Steerforth showed his consideration in one particular instance, in an unflinching manner that was a little tantalizing, I suspect, to poor Traddles and the rest. Peggotty's promised letter—what a comfortable letter it was!—arrived before "the half" was many weeks old; and with it a cake in a perfect nest of oranges, and two bottles of cowslip wine. This treasure, as in duty bound, I laid at the feet of Steerforth, and begged him to dispense.

"Now, I'll tell you what, young Copperfield," said he, "the wine shall be kept to wet your whistle when you are story-telling."

I blushed at the idea, and begged him, in my modesty, not to think of it. But he said he had observed I was sometimes hoarse—a little roopy was his exact expression—and it should be, every drop, devoted to the purpose he had mentioned. Accordingly, it was locked up in his box, and drawn off by himself in a phial, and administered to me through a piece of quill in the cork, when I was supposed to be in want of a restorative. Sometimes, to make it a more sovereign specific, he was so kind as to squeeze orange juice into it, or to stir it up with ginger, or dissolve a peppermint drop in it.

We seem to me to have been months over Peregrine, and months more over the other stories. The institution never flagged for want of a story, I am certain; and the wine lasted out almost as well as the matter. Poor Traddles—I never think of that boy but with a strange disposition to laugh, and with tears in my eyes—was a sort of chorus, in general; and affected to be convulsed with mirth at the comic parts, and to be overcome with fear when there was any passage of an alarming character in the narrative. This rather put me out, very often. It was a great jest of his, I recollect, to pretend that he couldn't keep his teeth from chattering, whenever mention was made of an Alguazil in connection with the adventures of Gil Blas; and I remember when Gil Blas met the captain of the robbers in Madrid, this unlucky joker counterfeited such an ague of terror that he was overheard by Mr. Creakle, who was prowling about the passage, and handsomely flogged for disorderly conduct in the bedroom.

One day I had a visit from Mr. Peggotty and Ham, who had brought two enormous lobsters, a huge crab, and a large canvas bag of shrimps, as they "remembered I was partial to a relish with my meals."

LITTLE DAVID COPPERFIELD.

I was proud to introduce my friend Steerforth to these kind, simple friends, and told them how good Steerforth was to me, and how he helped me with my work and took care of me, and Steerforth delighted the fishermen with his friendly, pleasant manners.

The "relish" was much appreciated by the boys at supper that night. Only poor Traddles became very ill from eating crab so late.

At last the holidays came, and I went home. The carrier, Barkis, met me at Yarmouth, and was rather gruff, which I soon found out was because he had not had any answer to his message. I promised to ask Peggotty for one.

Ah, what a strange feeling it was to be going home when it was not home, and to find that every object I looked at reminded me of the happy old home, which was like a dream I could never dream again!

God knows how infantine the memory may have been that was awakened within me by the sound of my mother's voice in the old parlor, when I set foot in the hall.

I believed, from the solitary and thoughtful way in which my mother murmured her song, that she was alone. And I went softly into the room. She was sitting by the fire, nursing an infant, whose tiny hand she held against her neck. Her eyes were looking down upon its face, and she sat singing to it. I was so far right, that she had no other companion.

I spoke to her, and she started, and cried out. But seeing me, she called me her dear Davy, her own boy; and, coming half across the room to meet me, kneeled down upon the ground and kissed me, and laid my head down on her bosom near the little creature that was nestling there, and put its hand up to my lips.

I wish I had died. I wish I had died then, with that feeling in my heart! I should have been more fit for heaven than I ever have been since.

"He is your brother," said my mother, fondling me. "Davy, my pretty boy! My poor child!" Then she kissed me more and more, and clasped me round the neck. This she was doing when Peggotty came running in, and bounced down on the ground beside us and went mad about us both for a quarter of an hour.

We had a very happy afternoon the day I came. Mr. and Miss Murd-

LITTLE DAVID COPPERFIELD.

stone were out, and I sat with my mother and Peggotty, and told them all about my school and Steerforth, and took the little baby in my arms and nursed it lovingly. But when the Murdstones came back I was more unhappy than ever.

I felt uncomfortable about going down to breakfast in the morning, as I had never set eyes on Mr. Murdstone since the day when I committed my memorable offense. However, as it must be done, I went down, after two or three false starts half-way, and as many runs back on tiptoe to my own room, and presented myself in the parlor.

He was standing before the fire with his back to it, while Miss Murdstone made the tea. He looked at me steadily as I entered, but made no sign of recognition whatever.

I went up to him, after a moment of confusion, and said, "I beg your pardon, sir. I am very sorry for what I did, and I hope you will forgive me."

"I am glad to hear you are sorry, David," he replied.

The hand he gave me was the hand I had bitten. I could not restrain my eye from resting for an instant on a red spot upon it.

"How do you do, ma'am?" I said to Miss Murdstone.

"Ah, dear me!" sighed Miss Murdstone, giving me the tea-caddy scoop instead of her fingers. "How long are the holidays?"

"A month, ma'am."

"Counting from when?"

"From to-day, ma'am."

"Oh!" said Miss Murdstone. "Then here's *one* day off."

She kept a calendar of the holidays in this way, and every morning checked a day off in exactly the same manner. She did it gloomily until she came to ten, but when she got into two figures she became more hopeful, and, as the time advanced, even jocular.

Thus the holidays lagged away, until the morning came when Miss Murdstone said: "Here's the last day off!" and gave me the closing cup of tea of the vacation.

I was not sorry to go. Again Mr. Barkis appeared at the gate, and again Miss Murdstone in her warning voice said: "Clara!" when my mother bent over me, to bid me farewell.

I kissed her and my baby brother; it is not so much the embrace she

106

gave me that lives in my mind, though it was as fervent as could be, as what followed the embrace.

I was in the carrier's cart when I heard her calling to me. I looked out, and she stood at the garden gate alone, holding her baby up in her arms for me to see. It was cold, still weather; and not a hair of her head, or fold of her dress, was stirred, as she looked intently at me, holding up her child.

So I lost her. So I saw her afterwards, in my sleep at school—a silent presence near my bed—looking at me with the same intent face—holding up her baby in her arms.

About two months after I had been back at school I was sent for one day to go into the parlor. I hurried in joyfully, for it was my birthday, and I thought it might be a hamper from Peggotty—but, alas! no; it was very sad news Mrs. Creakle had to give me—my dear mamma had died! Mrs. Creakle was very kind and gentle to me, and the boys, especially Traddles, were very sorry for me.

I went home the next day, and heard that the dear baby had died too. Peggotty received me with great tenderness, and told me about my mother's illness and how she had sent a loving message to me.

"Tell my dearest boy that his mother, as she lay here, blessed him not once, but a thousand times," and she had prayed to God to protect and keep her fatherless boy.

Mr. Murdstone did not take any notice of me, nor had Miss Murdstone a word of kindness for me. Peggotty was to leave in a month, and, to my great joy, I was allowed to go with her on a visit to Mr. Peggotty. On our way I found out that the mysterious message I had given to Peggotty meant that Barkis wanted to marry her, and Peggotty had consented. Everyone in Mr. Peggotty's cottage was pleased to see me, and did their best to comfort me. Little Em'ly was at school when I arrived, and I went out to meet her. I knew the way by which she would come, and presently found myself strolling along the path to meet her.

A figure appeared in the distance before long, and I soon knew it to be Em'ly, who was a little creature still in stature, though she was grown. But when she drew nearer, and I saw her blue eyes looking bluer, and her dimpled face looking brighter, and her own self prettier and gayer, a curious feeling came over me that made me pretend not to know her, and pass by as if I were looking at something a long way off. I have done such a thing since in later life, or I am mistaken.

Little Em'ly didn't care a bit. She saw me well enough; but instead of turning round and calling after me, ran away laughing. This obliged me to run after her, and she ran so fast that we were very near the cottage before I caught her.

"Oh, it's you, is it?" said little Em'ly.

"Why, you knew who it was, Em'ly," said I.

"And didn't *you* know who it was?" said Em'ly. I was going to kiss her, but she covered her cherry lips with her hands, and said she wasn't a baby now, and ran away, laughing more than ever, into the house.

She seemed to delight in teasing me, which was a change in her I wondered at very much. The tea-table was ready, and our little locker was put out in its old place, but instead of coming to sit by me, she went and bestowed her company upon that grumbling Mrs. Gummidge; and on Mr. Peggotty's inquiring why, rumpled her hair all over her face to hide it, and would do nothing but laugh.

"A little puss it is!" said Mr. Peggotty, patting her with his great hand.

"Ah," said Mr. Peggotty, running his fingers through her bright curls, "here's another orphan, you see, sir, and here," giving Ham a backhanded knock in the chest, "is another of 'em, though he don't look much like it."

"If I had *you* for a guardian, Mr. Peggotty," said I, "I don't think I should *feel* much like it."

Em'ly was confused by our all observing her, and hung down her head, and her face was covered with blushes. Glancing up presently through her stray curls, and seeing that we were all looking at her still (I am sure I, for one, could have looked at her for hours), she ran away, and kept away till it was nearly bedtime.

I lay down in the old little bed in the stern of the boat, and the wind came moaning on across the flat as it had done before. But I could not help fancying, now, that it moaned of those who were gone; and instead of thinking that the sea might rise in the night and float the boat away, I thought of the sea that had risen, since I last heard those sounds, and drowned my happy home. I recollect, as the wind and water began to sound fainter in my ears, putting a short clause into my prayers, petitioning that I might grow up to marry little Em'ly, and so dropping lovingly asleep.

During this visit Peggotty was married to Mr. Barkis, and had a nice little house of her own, and I spent the night before I was to return home in a little room in the roof.

"Young or old, Davy dear, so long as I have this house over my head," said Peggotty, "you shall find it as if I expected you here directly every minute. I shall keep it as I used to keep your old little room, my darling, and if you was to go to China, you might think of its being kept just the same all the time you were away."

I felt how good and true a friend she was, and thanked her as well as I could, for they had brought me to the gate of my home, and Peggotty had me clasped in her arms.

I was poor and lonely at home, with no one near to speak a loving word, or a face to look on with love or liking, only the two persons who had broken my mother's heart. How utterly wretched and forlorn I felt! I found I was not to go back to school any more, and wandered about sad and solitary, neglected and uncared for. Peggotty's weekly visits were my only comfort. I longed to go to school, however hard an one, to be taught something anyhow, anywhere—but no one took any pains with me, and I had no friends near who could help me.

At last one day, after some weary months had passed, Mr. Murdstone told me I was to go to London and earn my own living. There was a place for me at Murdstone & Grinby's, a firm in the wine trade. My lodging and clothes would be provided for me by my step-father, and I would earn enough for my food and pocket money. The next day, I was sent up to London with the manager, dressed in a shabby little white hat with black crape round it for my mother, a black jacket, and hard, stiff corduroy trousers, a little fellow of ten years old, to fight my own battles with the world!

My place, I found, was one of the lowest in the firm of Murdstone & Grinby, with boys of no education and in quite an inferior station to myself—my duties were to wash the bottles, stick on labels, and so on. I was utterly miserable at being degraded in this way, when I thought of my former companions, Steerforth and Traddles, and my hopes of becoming a learned and distinguished man, and shed bitter tears, as I feared I would forget all I had learnt at school. My lodging, one bare little room, was in the house of some people named Micawber, shiftless, careless, good-natured people, who were always in debt and difficulties. I felt great pity for their misfortunes and did what I could to help poor Mrs. Micawber to sell her books and other little things she could spare, to buy food for herself, her husband, and their four children. I was too young and childish to know how to provide properly for myself, and often found I was obliged to live on bread and slices of cold pudding at the end of the week. If I had not been a very innocent-minded, good little boy, I might easily have fallen into bad ways at this time. But God took care of me and kept me from harm. I would not even tell Peggotty how miserable I was, for fear of distressing her.

The troubles of the Micawbers increased more and more, until at last they were obliged to leave London. I was very sad at this, for I had been with them so long that I felt they were my friends, and the prospect of being once more utterly alone, and having to find a lodging with strangers, made me so unhappy that I determined to endure this sort of life no longer. The last Sunday the Micawbers were in town I dined with them. I had bought a spotted horse for their little boy and a doll for the little girl, and had saved up a shilling for the poor servant-girl. After I had seen them off the next morning by the coach, I wrote to Peggotty to ask her if she knew where my aunt, Miss Betsy Trotwood, lived, and to borrow half-a-guinea; for I had resolved to run away from Murdstone & Grinby's, and go to this aunt and tell her my story. I remembered my mother telling me of her visit when I was a baby, and that she fancied Miss Betsy had stroked her hair gently, and this gave me courage to appeal to her. Peggotty wrote, enclosing the half-guinea, and saying she only knew Miss Trotwood lived near Dover, but whether in that place itself, or at Folkestone, Sandgate, or Hythe, she could not tell. Hearing that all these places were close together, I made up my mind to start. As I had received my week's wages in advance, I waited till the following Saturday, thinking it would not be honest to go before. I went out to look for someone to carry my box to the coach office, and unfortunately employed a wicked young man who not only ran off with the box, but robbed me of my half-guinea, leaving me in dire distress.

In despair, I started off to walk to Dover, and was forced to sell my waistcoat to buy some bread. The first night I found my way to my old school at Blackheath, and slept on a haystack close by, feeling some comfort in the thought of the boys being near. I knew Steerforth had left, or I would have tried to see him.

On I trudged the next day and sold my jacket at Chatham to a dreadful old man, who kept me waiting all day for the money, which was only one shilling and fourpence. I was afraid to buy anything but bread or to spend any money on a bed or a shelter for the night, and was terribly frightened by some rough tramps, who threw stones at me when I did not answer to their calls. After six days, I arrived at Dover, ragged, dusty, and half-dead with hunger and fatigue. But here, at first, I could get no tidings of my aunt, and, in despair, was going to try some of the other places Peggotty had mentioned, when the driver of a fly dropped his horsecloth, and as I was handing it up to him, I saw something kind in the man's face that encouraged me to ask once more if he knew where Miss Trotwood lived.

The man directed me towards some houses on the heights, and thither I toiled. Going into a little shop, I by chance met with Miss Trotwood's maid, who showed me the house, and went in leaving me standing at the gate, a forlorn little creature, without a jacket or waistcoat, my white hat crushed out of shape, my shoes worn out, my shirt and trousers torn and stained, my pretty curly hair tangled, my face and hands sunburnt and covered with dust. Lifting my eyes to one of the windows above, I saw a pleasant-faced gentleman with gray hair, who nodded at me several times, then shook his head and went away. I was just turning away to think what I should do, when a tall, erect elderly lady, with a gardening apron on and a knife in her hand, came out of the house, and began to dig up a root in the garden.

"Go away," she said. "Go away. No boys here."

But I felt desperate. Going in softly, I stood beside her, and touched her with my finger, and said timidly, "If you please, ma'am——" and when she looked up, I went on—

"Please, aunt, I am your nephew."

"Oh, Lord!" she exclaimed in astonishment, and sat flat down on the path, staring at me, while I went on—

LITTLE DAVID COPPERFIELD.

"I am David Copperfield of Blunderstone, in Suffolk, where you came the night I was born, and saw my dear mamma. I have been very unhappy since she died. I have been slighted and taught nothing, and thrown upon myself, and put to work not fit for me. It made me run away to you. I was robbed at first starting out and have walked all the way, and have never slept in a bed since I began the journey." Here I broke into a passion of crying, and my aunt jumped up and took

"WELL, IF I WAS YOU, I SHOULD WASH HIM," SAID MR. DICK.

me into the house, where she opened a cupboard and took out some bottles, pouring some of the contents of each into my mouth, not noticing in her agitation what they were, for I fancied I tasted anise-seed water, anchovy sauce, and salad dressing! Then she put me on the sofa and sent the servant to ask "Mr. Dick" to come down. The gentleman whom I had seen at the window came in and was told by Miss Trotwood who the ragged little object on the sofa was, and she finished by saying—

LITTLE DAVID COPPERFIELD.

"Now here you see young David Copperfield, and the question is what shall I do with him?"

"Do with him?" answered Mr. Dick. Then, after some consideration, and looking at me, he said, "Well, if I was you, I should wash him!"

Miss Trotwood was quite pleased at this, and a warm bath was got ready at once, after which I was dressed in a shirt and trousers belonging to Mr. Dick (for Janet had burnt my rags), rolled up in several shawls, and put on the sofa till dinner-time, where I slept, and woke with the impression that my aunt had come and put my hair off my face, and murmured, "Pretty fellow, poor fellow."

After dinner I had to tell my story all over again to my aunt and Mr. Dick. Miss Trotwood again asked Mr. Dick's advice, and was delighted when that gentleman suggested I should be put to bed. I knelt down to say my prayers that night in a pleasant room facing the sea, and as I lay in the clean, snow-white bed, I felt so grateful and comforted that I prayed earnestly I might never be homeless again, and might never forget the homeless.

The next morning my aunt told me she had written to Mr. Murdstone. I was alarmed to think that my step-father knew where I was, and exclaimed—

"Oh, I don't know what I shall do if I have to go back to Mr. Murdstone!"

But my aunt said nothing of her intentions, and I was uncertain what was to become of me. I hoped she might befriend me.

At last Mr. and Miss Murdstone arrived. To Miss Betsy's great indignation, Miss Murdstone rode a donkey across the green in front of the house, and stopped at the gate. Nothing made Miss Trotwood so angry as to see donkeys on that green, and I had already seen several battles between my aunt or Janet and the donkey boys.

After driving away the donkey and the boy who had dared to bring it there, Miss Trotwood received her visitors. She kept me near her, fenced in with a chair.

Mr. Murdstone told Miss Betsy that I was a very bad, stubborn, violent-tempered boy, whom he had tried to improve, but could not succeed; that he had put me in a respectable business from which I had run away. If Miss Trotwood chose to protect and encourage me now, she must do it always, for he had come to fetch me away there and then, and if I was not ready to come, and Miss Trotwood did not wish to give me up to be dealt with exactly as Mr. Murdstone liked, he would cast me off for always, and have no more to do with me.

"Are you ready to go, David?" asked my aunt.

But I answered no, and begged and prayed her for my father's sake to befriend and protect me, for neither Mr. nor Miss Murdstone had ever liked me or been kind to me and had made my mamma, who always loved me dearly, very unhappy about me, and I had been very miserable.

"Mr. Dick," said Miss Trotwood, "what shall I do with this child?"

Mr. Dick considered. "Have him measured for a suit of clothes directly."

"Mr. Dick," said Miss Trotwood, "your commonsense is invaluable."

Then she pulled me towards her, and said to Mr. Murdstone, "You can go when you like. I'll take my chance with the boy. If he's all you say he is I can at least do as much for him as you have done. But I don't believe a word of it."

Then she told Mr. Murdstone what she thought of the way he had treated me and my mother, which did not make that gentleman feel very comfortable, and finished by turning to Miss Murdstone and saying—

"Good-day to you, too, ma'am, and if I ever see you ride a donkey across my green again, as sure as you have a head upon your shoulders, I'll knock your bonnet off and tread upon it!"

This startled Miss Murdstone so much that she went off quite quietly with her brother, while I, overjoyed, threw my arms round my aunt's neck, and kissed and thanked her with great heartiness.

Some clothes were bought for me that same day and marked "Trotwood Copperfield," for my aunt wished to call me by her name.

Now I felt my troubles were over, and I began quite a new life, well cared for and kindly treated. I was sent to a very nice school in Canterbury, where my aunt left me with these words, which I never forgot:

"Trot, be a credit to yourself, to me, and Mr. Dick, and heaven be with you. Never be mean in anything, never be false, never be cruel. Avoid these three vices, Trot, and I shall always be hopeful of you?"

I did my best to show my gratitude to my dear aunt by studying hard, and trying to be all she could wish.

When you are older you can read how Little David Copperfield grew up to be a good, clever man, and met again all his old friends, and made many new ones.

Also, what became of Steerforth, Traddles, the Peggottys, little Em'ly, and the Micawbers.

A Brave and Honest Boy, Oliver Twist.

LITTLE OLIVER TWIST was an orphan. He never saw his mother or his father. He was born at the workhouse, where his poor heart-broken mother had been taken just a short time before baby Oliver came; and, the very night he was born, she was so sick and weak she said: "Let me see my child and then I will die." The old nurse said: "Nonsense, my dear, you must not think of dying, you have something now to live for." The good kind doctor said she must be very brave and she might get well. They brought her little baby boy to her, and she hugged him in her weak arms and she kissed him on the brow many times and cuddled him up as close as her feeble arms could hold him; and then she looked at him long and steadily, and a sweet smile came over her face and a bright light came into her eyes, and before the smile could pass from her lips she died.

The old nurse wept as she took the little baby from its dead mother's arms; and the good doctor had to wipe the tears from his eyes, it was so very, very sad.

After wrapping the baby in a blanket and laying him in a warm place, the old nurse straightened out the limbs of the young mother and folded her hands on her breast; and, spreading a white sheet over her still form, she called the doctor to look at her—for the nurse and the doctor were all who were there. The same sweet smile was on her face, and the doctor said as he looked upon her: "Poor, poor girl, she is so beautiful and so young! What strange fate has brought her to this poor place? Nurse, take good care of the baby, for his mother must have been, at one time, a kind and gentle woman."

The next day they took the unknown woman out to the potter's field and buried her; and, for nine months, the old nurse at the workhouse took care of the baby; though, it is sad to say, this old woman, kind-hearted though she was, was at the same time so fond of gin that she often took the money, which ought to have bought milk for the baby, to buy drink for herself.

Nobody knew what the young mother's name was, and so this baby had no name, until, at last, Mr. Bumble, who was one of the parish officers who looked after the paupers, came and named him *Oliver Twist.*

When little Oliver was nine months old they took him away from the workhouse and carried him to the "Poor Farm," where there were twenty-five or thirty other poor children who had no parents. A woman by the name of Mrs. Mann had charge of this cottage. The parish gave her an allowance of enough money to keep the children in plenty of food and clothing; but she starved the little ones to keep the money for herself, so that many of them died and others came to take their places. But young Oliver was a tough little fellow, and, while he looked very pale and thin, he was, otherwise, healthy and hung on to his life.

Mrs. Mann was also very cruel to the children. She would scold and beat them and shut them up in the cellar and treat them mean in many ways when no visitors were there. But, when any of the men who had control or visitors came around, she would smile and call the children "dear," and all sorts of pet names. She told them if any of them should tell on her she would beat them; and, furthermore, that they should tell visitors that she was very kind and good to them and that they loved her very much.

Mr. Bumble was a very mean man, too, as we shall see. They called him the *Beadle,* which means he was a sort of sheriff or policeman; and he was supposed to look after the people at the workhouse and at the poor farm and to wait on the directors who had charge of these places. He had the right to punish the boys if they did not mind, and they were all afraid of him.

Oliver remained at the cottage on the poor farm until he was nine years old, though he was a little pale fellow and did not look to be over seven.

On the morning of his birthday, Mrs. Mann had given Oliver and two other boys a bad whipping and put them down in a dark coal-cellar. Presently she saw Mr. Bumble coming and she told her servant to take the boys out and wash them quick, for she did not let Mr. Bumble know she ever punished them and was fearful he might hear them crying in the dark, damp place. Mrs. Mann talked very nicely to Mr. Bumble and made him a "toddy," and kept him busy with her flattering and kindness until she knew the boys were washed.

Mr. Bumble told her Oliver Twist was nine years old that day, and the Board (which meant the men in charge) had decided they must take him away from the farm and carry him back to the workhouse. Mrs. Mann pretended to be very sorry, and she went out and brought Oliver in, telling him on the way that he must appear very sorry to leave her, otherwise she would beat him. So when Oliver was asked if he wanted to go, he said he was sorry to leave there. This was not a falsehood, for, miserable as the place was, he dearly loved his little companions. They were all the people he knew; and he did feel sad, and really wept with sorrow as he told them good-by and was led by Mr. Bumble back to the workhouse, where he was born and where his mother died nine years ago that very day.

When he got back there he found the old nurse who remembered his mother, and she told him she was a beautiful sweet woman and how she had kissed him and held him in her arms when she died. Night after night little Oliver dreamed about his beautiful mother, and she seemed sometimes to stand by his bed and to look down upon him with the same beautiful eyes and the same sweet smile of which the nurse told him. Every time he had the chance he asked questions about her, but the nurse could not tell him anything more. She did not even know her name.

Oliver had been at the workhouse only a very short time when Mr. Bumble came in and told him he must appear before the Board at once. Now Oliver was puzzled at this. He thought a board was a piece of flat wood, and he could not imagine why he was to appear before that. But he was too much afraid of Mr. Bumble to ask any questions. This gentleman had treated him roughly in bringing him to the workhouse; and, now, when he looked a little puzzled—for his expressive face always told what was in his honest little heart—Mr. Bumble gave him a sharp crack on the head with his cane and another rap over the back and told him to wake up and not look so sleepy, and to mind to be polite when he went before the Board.   Oliver could not help tears coming into his eyes as he was pushed along, and Mr. Bumble gave him another sharp rap, telling him to hush, and ushered him into a room where several stern-looking gentlemen sat at a long table.   One of them, in a white waistcoat, was particularly mean-looking.   " Bow to the Board," said Mr. Bumble to Oliver.   Oliver looked about for a board, and, seeing none, he bowed to the table, because it looked more like a board than anything else. The men laughed, and the man in the white waistcoat said: " The boy is a fool.   I thought he was."   After other ugly remarks, they told Oliver he was an orphan and they had supported him all his life.   He ought to be very thankful.   (And he was, when he remembered how many had been starved to death.)   " Now," they said, " you are nine years old, and we must put you out to learn a trade."   They told him he should begin the next morning at six o'clock to pick oakum, and work at that until they could get him a place.

Oliver was faithful at his work, in which several other boys assisted, but oh ! so hungry they got, for they were given but one little bowl of gruel at a meal—hardly enough for a kitten.   So, one day the boys said they must ask for more; and they " drew straws " to see who should venture to do so.   It fell to Oliver's lot to do it, and the next meal, when they had emptied their bowls, Oliver walked up to the man who helped them and said very politely, " Please, sir, may I not have some more ?   I am very hungry."   This made the man so angry that he hit Oliver over the head with his ladle and called for Mr. Bumble.   He came, and when told that Oliver had " asked for more," he grabbed him by the collar and took him before the Board and made the complaint that he had been very naughty and rebellious, telling the circumstance in an unfair and untruthful way.   The Board was angry at Oliver, and the man in the white waistcoat told them again the boy would be hung, and they must get rid of him at once.   So they offered twenty-five dollars to anyone who would take him.

The first man who came was a very mean chimney-sweeper, who had almost killed other boys with his mean treatment.   The Board agreed to let him have Oliver; but, when they took him before the magistrates, Oliver fell on his knees and begged them not to let that man have him, and they would not.   So Oliver was taken back to the workhouse.

A BRAVE AND HONEST BOY, OLIVER TWIST.

The next man who came was Mr. Sowerberry, an undertaker. He was a very good man, and the magistrates let him take Oliver along. But he had a very cross, stingy wife, and a mean servant-girl by the name of Charlotte, and a big overbearing boy by the name of Noah Claypole, whom he had taken to raise. Oliver thought he would like Mr. Sowerberry well enough, but his heart fell when " the Mrs." met him and called him "boy" and a "measly-looking little pauper," and gave him for supper the scraps she had put up for the dog. But this was so much better than he got at the workhouse, he would not complain about the food; and he hoped, by faithful work, to win kind treatment.

They made him sleep by himself in the shop among the coffins, and he was very much frightened; but he would rather sleep there than with that terrible boy, Noah. The first night he dreamed of his beautiful mother, and thought again he could see her sitting among those black, fearful coffins, with the same sweet smile upon her face. He was awakened the next morning by Noah, who told him he had to obey him, and he'd better lookout or he'd wear the life out of him. Noah kicked and cuffed Oliver several times, but the poor boy was too much used to that to resent it, and determined to do his work well.

Mr. Sowerberry found Oliver so good, sensible, and polite that he made him his assistant and took him to all the funerals, and occasionally gave him a penny. Oliver went into fine houses and saw people and sights he had never dreamed of before. Mr. Sowerberry had told him he might some day be an undertaker himself; and Oliver worked hard to please his master, though Noah and Mrs. Sowerberry and Charlotte grew meaner to him all the time, because " he was put forward," they said, " and Noah was kept back." This, of course, made Noah meaner than ever to Oliver—though Charlotte did sometimes try to make him less cruel—but Oliver determined to endure it all rather than complain, and try to win them over after awhile by being kind. He could have borne any insult to himself, but Noah tried the little fellow too far when he attacked the name of Oliver's mother, and it brought serious trouble, as we shall see.

One day, Oliver and Noah had descended into the kitchen at the usual dinner-hour, when, Charlotte being called out of the way, there ensued a brief interval of time, which Noah Claypole, being hungry and vicious, considered he could not possibly devote to a worthier purpose than aggravating and tantalizing young Oliver Twist.

Intent upon this innocent amusement, Noah put his feet on the table-cloth; and pulled Oliver's hair; and twitched his ears; and expressed his opinion that he was a "sneak;" and furthermore announced his intention of coming to see him hanged, whenever that desirable event should take place; and entered upon various other topics of petty annoyance, like a malicious and ill-conditioned charity-boy as he was. But, none of these taunts producing the desired effect of making Oliver cry, Noah began to talk about his mother.

"Work'us," said Noah, "how's your mother?"

"She's dead," replied Oliver; "don't you say anything about her to me!"

Oliver's color rose as he said this; he breathed quickly; and there was a curious working of the mouth and nostrils, which Noah thought must be the immediate precursor of a violent fit of crying. Under this impression he returned to the charge.

"What did she die of, Work'us?" said Noah.

"Of a broken-heart, some of our old nurses told me," replied Oliver: more as if he were talking to himself than answering Noah. "I think I know what it must be to die of that!"

"Tol de rol lol lol, right fol lairy, Work'us," said Noah, as a tear rolled down Oliver's cheek. "What's set you a sniveling now?"

"Not *you*," replied Oliver, hastily brushing the tear away. "Don't think it."

"Oh, not me, eh?" sneered Noah.

"No, not you," replied Oliver, sharply. "There, that's enough. Don't say anything more to me about her; you'd better not!"

"Better not!" exclaimed Noah. "Well! Better not! Work'us, don't be impudent. *Your* mother, too! She was a nice 'un, she was. Oh, Lor'!" And here Noah nodded his head expressively and curled his small red nose.

"Yer know, Work'us," continued Noah, emboldened by Oliver's silence, and speaking in a jeering tone of affected pity. "Yer know, Work'us, it can't be helped now; and of course yer couldn't help it then. But yer must know, Work'us, yer mother was a regular right-down bad 'un."

"What did you say?" inquired Oliver, looking up very quickly.

"A regular right-down bad 'un, Work'us," replied Noah, coolly. "And it's a great deal better, Work'us, that she died when she did, or else she'd have been hard laboring in Bridewell, or transported, or hung; which is more likely than either, isn't it?"

Crimson with fury, Oliver started up; overthrew the chair and table; seized Noah by the throat; shook him, in the violence of his rage, till his teeth chattered in his head; and, collecting his whole force into one heavy blow, felled him to the ground.

A minute ago, the boy had looked the quiet, mild, dejected creature that harsh treatment had made him. But his spirit was roused at last; the cruel insult to his dead mother had set his blood on fire. His breast heaved; his attitude was erect; his eye bright and vivid; his whole person changed, as he stood glaring over the cowardly tormentor who now lay crouching at his feet; and defied him with an energy he had never known before.

"He'll murder me!" blubbered Noah. "Charlotte! missis! Here's the new boy a-murdering of me! Help! help! Oliver's gone mad! Char—lotte!"

Noah's shouts were responded to by a loud scream from Charlotte and a louder from Mrs. Sowerberry; the former of whom rushed into the kitchen by a side-door, while the latter paused on the staircase till she was quite certain that it was safe to come farther down.

"Oh, you little wretch!" screamed Charlotte, seizing Oliver with her utmost force, which was about equal to that of a moderately strong man in particularly good training. "Oh, you little un-grate-ful, mur-de-rous, hor-rid villain!" And between every syllable Charlotte gave Oliver a blow with all her might.

Charlotte's fist was by no means a light one; and Mrs. Sowerberry plunged into the kitchen and assisted to hold him with one hand, while she scratched his face with the other. In this favorable position of affairs, Noah rose from the ground and pommeled him behind.

When they were all wearied out, and could tear and beat no longer, they dragged Oliver, struggling and shouting, but nothing daunted, into the dust-cellar, and there locked him up. This being done, Mrs. Sowerberry sunk into a chair and burst into tears.

"Oh! Charlotte," said Mrs. Sowerberry. "Oh! Charlotte, what a mercy we have not all been murdered in our beds!"

"Ah! mercy indeed, ma'am," was the reply. "I only hope this'll teach master not to have any more of these dreadful creaturs, that are born to be murderers and robbers from their very cradle. Poor Noah! he was all but killed, ma'am, when I come in."

"Poor fellow!" said Mrs. Sowerberry, looking piteously on the charity-boy.

OLIVER RATHER ASTONISHES NOAH.

"What's to be done!" exclaimed Mrs. Sowerberry. "Your master's not at home; there's not a man in the house, and he'll kick that door down in ten minutes." Oliver's vigorous plunges against the door did seem as if he would break it.

"Dear, dear! I don't know, ma'am," said Charlotte, "unless we send for the police officers."

"Or the millingtary," suggested Noah.

"No, no," said Mrs. Sowerberry: bethinking herself of Oliver's old friend. "Run to Mr. Bumble, Noah, and tell him to come here directly, and not to lose a minute; never mind your cap! Make haste!"

Noah set off with all his might, and paused not once for breath until he reached the workhouse gate.

"Why, what's the matter with the boy!" said the people as Noah rushed up.

"Mr. Bumble! Mr. Bumble!" cried Noah, with well-affected dismay. "Oh, Mr. Bumble, sir! Oliver, sir—Oliver has—"

"What? What?" interposed Mr. Bumble, with a gleam of pleasure in his metallic eyes. "Not run away; he hasn't run away, has he, Noah?"

"No, sir, no. Not run away, sir, but he's turned wicious," replied Noah. "He tried to murder me, sir; and then he tried to murder Charlotte; and then missis. Oh! what dreadful pain it is! Such agony, please, sir!" And here Noah writhed and twisted his body into an extensive variety of eel-like positions, by which the gentleman's notice was very soon attracted; for he had not walked three paces, when he turned angrily round and inquired what that young cur was howling for.

"It's a poor boy from the free-school, sir," replied Mr. Bumble, "who has been nearly murdered—all but murdered, sir—by young Twist."

"By Jove!" exclaimed the gentleman in the white waistcoat, stopping short. "I knew it! I felt from the very first that that audacious young savage would come to be hung!"

"He has likewise attempted, sir, to murder the female servant," said Mr. Bumble, with a face of ashy paleness.

"And his missis," interposed Noah.

"And his master, too, I think you said, Noah?" added Mr. Bumble.

"No! he's out, or he would have murdered him," replied Noah. "He said he wanted to."

"Ah! Said he wanted to, did he, my boy?" inquired the gentleman in the white waistcoat.

"Yes, sir. And please, sir," replied Noah, "missis wants to know whether Mr. Bumble can spare time to step up there, directly, and flog him—'cause master's out."

"Certainly, my boy; certainly," said the gentleman in the white waistcoat, smiling benignly and patting Noah's head, which was about three inches higher than his own. "You're a good boy—a very good boy. Here's a penny for you. Bumble, just step up to Sowerberry's with your cane, and see what's to be done. Don't spare him, Bumble."

"No, I will not, sir," replied the beadle as he hurried away.

Meantime, Oliver continued to kick, with undiminished vigor, at the cellar-door. The accounts of his ferocity, as related by Mrs. Sowerberry and Charlotte, were of so startling a nature that Mr. Bumble judged it prudent to parley before opening the door. With this view he gave a kick at the outside, by way of prelude; and then, applying his mouth to the keyhole, said, in a deep and impressive tone:

"Oliver!"

"Come, you let me out!" replied Oliver, from the inside.

"Do you know this here voice, Oliver?" said Mr. Bumble.

"Yes," replied Oliver.

"Ain't you afraid of it, sir? Ain't you a-trembling while I speak, sir?" said Mr. Bumble.

"No!" replied Oliver, boldly.

An answer so different from the one he had expected to elicit, and was in the habit of receiving, staggered Mr. Bumble not a little.

"Oh, you know, Mr. Bumble, he must be mad," said Mrs. Sowerberry. "No boy in half his senses could venture to speak so to you."

"It's not madness, ma'am," replied Mr. Bumble, after a few moments of deep meditation. "It's meat."

"What?" exclaimed Mrs. Sowerberry.

"Meat, ma'am, meat," replied Bumble, with stern emphasis. "You've overfed him, ma'am."

"Dear, dear!" ejaculated Mrs. Sowerberry, piously raising her eyes to the kitchen ceiling; "this comes of being liberal!"

The liberality of Mrs. Sowerberry to Oliver had consisted in a profuse bestowal upon him of all the dirty odds and ends which nobody else would eat.

"Ah!" said Mr. Bumble, when the lady brought her eyes down to earth again; "the only thing that can be done now, that I know of, is to leave him in the cellar for a day or so, till he's a little starved down; and then to take him out, and keep him on gruel all through his apprenticeship. He comes of a bad family. Excitable natures, Mrs. Sowerberry! Both the nurse and doctor said that that mother of his made her way here, against difficulties and pain that would have killed any well-disposed woman, weeks before."

At this point of Mr. Bumble's discourse, Oliver, just hearing enough to know that some new allusion was being made to his mother, recommenced kicking, with a violence that rendered every other sound inaudible. Sowerberry returned at this juncture. Oliver's offense having been explained to him, with such exaggerations as the ladies thought best calculated to rouse his ire, he unlocked the cellar-door in a twinkling, and dragged his rebellious apprentice out by the collar.

Oliver's clothes had been torn in the beating he had received; his face was bruised and scratched; and his hair scattered over his forehead. The angry flush had not disappeared, however; and when he was pulled out of his prison, he scowled boldly on Noah, and looked quite undismayed.

"Now, you are a nice young fellow, ain't you?" said Sowerberry, giving Oliver a shake and a box on the ear.

"He called my mother names," replied Oliver.

"Well, and what if he did, you little ungrateful wretch?" said Mrs. Sowerberry. "She deserved what he said, and worse."

"She didn't," said Oliver.

"She did," said Mrs. Sowerberry.

"It's a lie!" said Oliver.

Mrs. Sowerberry burst into a flood of tears.

This flood of tears left Mr. Sowerberry no alternative; so he at once gave Oliver a drubbing, which satisfied even Mrs. Sowerberry herself. For the rest of the day he was shut up in the back kitchen, in company with a pump and a slice of bread; and, at night, Mrs. Sowerberry, after making various remarks outside the door, by no means complimentary to the memory of his mother, looked into the room, and, amidst the jeers and pointings of Noah and Charlotte, ordered him up stairs to his dismal bed.

It was not until he was left alone in the silence and stillness of the gloomy workshop of the undertaker that Oliver gave way to the feelings which the day's treatment may be supposed likely to have awakened in a mere child. He had listened to their taunts with a look of contempt;

he had borne the lash without a cry; for he felt that pride swelling in his heart which would have kept down a shriek to the last, though they had roasted him alive. But now, when there was none to see or hear him, he fell upon his knees on the floor; and, hiding his face in his hands, wept bitter tears and prayed in his bleeding heart that God would help him to get away from these cruel people. There upon his knees Oliver determined to run away, and, rising, tied up a few clothes in a handkerchief and went to bed.

With the first ray of light that struggled through the crevices in the shutters, Oliver arose and unbarred the door. One timid look around—one moment's pause of hesitation—he had closed it behind him, and was in the open street.

He looked to the right and to the left, uncertain which way to fly. He remembered to have seen the wagons, as they went out, toiling up the hill. He took the same route; and arriving at a foot-path across the fields, which he knew, after some distance, led out again into the road, struck into it, and walked quickly on.

Along this same foot-path, Oliver well remembered he had trotted beside Mr. Bumble, when he first carried him to the workhouse from the farm. His heart beat quickly when he bethought himself of this, and he half resolved to turn back. He had come a long way though, and should lose a great deal of time by doing so. Besides, it was so early that there was very little fear of his being seen; so he walked on.

He reached the house. There was no appearance of its inmates stirring at that early hour. Oliver stopped, and peeped into the garden. A child was weeding one of the little beds; as he stopped, he raised his pale face and disclosed the features of one of his former companions. Oliver felt glad to see him before he went; for, though younger than himself, he had been his little friend and playmate. They had been beaten, and starved, and shut up together many and many a time.

"Hush, Dick!" said Oliver, as the boy ran to the gate, and thrust his thin arm between the rails to greet him. "Is anyone up?"

"Nobody but me," replied the child.

"You mustn't say you saw me, Dick," said Oliver. "I am running away. They beat and ill-use me, Dick; and I am going to seek my fortune some long way off. I don't know where. How pale you are!"

"I heard the doctor tell them I was dying," replied the child, with a faint smile. "I am very glad to see you, dear; but don't stop, don't stop!"

"Yes, yes, I will, to say good-by to you," replied Oliver. "I shall see you again, Dick. I know I shall. You will be well and happy!"

"I hope so," replied the child. "After I am dead, but not before. I know the doctor must be right, Oliver, because I dream so much of heaven, and angels, and kind faces that I never see when I am awake. Kiss me," said the child, climbing up the low gate, and flinging his little arms around Oliver's neck: "Good-by, dear! God bless you!"

The blessing was from a young child's lips, but it was the first that Oliver had ever heard invoked upon his head; and through the struggles and sufferings, and troubles and changes of his after-life, he never once forgot it.

Oliver soon got into the high-road. It was eight o'clock now. Though he was nearly five miles away from the town, he ran, and hid behind the hedges, by turns, till noon, fearing that he might be pursued and overtaken. Then he sat down to rest by the side of the mile-stone.

The stone by which he was seated had a sign on it which said that it was just seventy miles from that spot to London. The name awakened a new train of ideas in the boy's mind. London!—that great large place!—nobody—not even Mr. Bumble—could ever find him there! He had often heard the old men in the workhouse, too, say that no lad of spirit need want in London; and that there were ways of living in that vast city which those who had been bred in the country parts had no idea of. It was the very place for a homeless boy, who must die in the streets unless someone helped him. As these things passed through his thoughts, he jumped upon his feet and again walked forward.

He had diminished the distance between himself and London by full four miles more, before he recollected how much he must undergo ere he could hope to reach his place of destination. As this consideration forced itself upon him, he slackened his pace a little, and meditated upon his means of getting there. He had a crust of bread, a coarse shirt, and two pairs of stockings in his bundle. He had a penny too—a gift of Sowerberry's after some funeral in which he had acquitted himself more than ordinarily well—in his pocket. "A clean shirt," thought Oliver, "is a very comfortable thing; and so are two pairs of darned stockings; and so is a penny; but they are small helps to a sixty-five miles' walk in winter-time."

Thus day after day the weary but plucky little boy walked on, and early on the seventh morning after he had left his native place, Oliver limped slowly into the little town of Barnet, and sat down on a doorstep to rest. Some few stopped to gaze at Oliver for a moment or two, or turned round to stare at him as they hurried by; but none relieved him, or troubled themselves to inquire how he came there. He had no heart to beg. And there he sat for some time when he was roused by observing that a boy was watching him most earnestly from the opposite side of the way. He took little heed of this at first; but the boy remained in the same attitude so long that Oliver raised his head and returned his steady look. Upon this, the boy crossed over, and, walking close up to Oliver, said:

"Hullo, my covey! What's the row?"

The boy who addressed this inquiry to the young wayfarer was about his own age: but one of the queerest-looking boys that Oliver had ever seen. He was a snub-nosed, flat-browed, common-faced boy enough; and as dirty a juvenile as one would wish to see; but he had about him all the airs and manners of a man. He was short for his age; with rather bow-legs, and little, sharp, ugly eyes. His hat was stuck on the top of his head so lightly that it threatened to fall off every moment. He wore a man's coat, which reached nearly to his heels.

"Hullo, my covey! What's the row?" said the stranger.

"I am very hungry and tired," replied Oliver: the tears standing in his eyes as he spoke. "I have walked a long way. I have been walking these seven days."

"Walking for sivin days!" said the young gentleman. "Oh, I see. Beak's order, eh? But," he added, noticing Oliver's look of surprise, "I suppose you don't know what a beak is, my flash com-pan-i-on."

Oliver mildly replied that he had always heard a bird's mouth described by the word beak.

"My eyes, how green!" exclaimed the young gentleman. "Why, a beak's a madgst'rate; and when you walk by a beak's order, it's not straight forerd.

"But come," said the young gentleman; "you want grub, and you shall have it. Up with you on your pins. There! Now then!"

Assisting Oliver to rise, the young gentleman took him to an adjacent grocery store, where he purchased a sufficiency of ready-dressed ham and a half-quartern loaf, or, as he himself expressed it, "a fourpenny bran!" Taking the bread under his arm, the young gentleman turned into a small public-house, and led the way to a tap-room in the rear of the premises. Here a pot of beer was brought in by direction of the mysterious youth; and Oliver, falling to at his new friend's bidding, made a long and hearty meal, during which the strange boy eyed him from time to time with great attention.

"Going to London?" said the strange boy, when Oliver had at length concluded.

"Yes."

"Got any lodgings?"

"No."

"Money?"

"No."

The strange boy whistled, and put his arms into his pockets as far as the big coat-sleeves would let them go.

"Do you live in London?" inquired Oliver.

"Yes, I do, when I'm at home," replied the boy. "I suppose you want some place to sleep in to-night, don't you?"

"I do, indeed," answered Oliver. "I have not slept under a roof since I left the country."

"Don't fret your eyelids on that score," said the young gentleman. "I've got to be in London to-night; and I know a 'spectable old genelman as lives there, wot'll give you lodgings for nothink, and never ask for the change—that is, if any genelman he knows interduces you. And don't he know me? Oh, no! not in the least! By no means. Certainly not!" which was his queer way of saying he and the old gentleman were good friends.

This unexpected offer of shelter was too tempting to be resisted, especially as it was immediately followed up by the assurance that the old gentleman referred to would doubtless provide Oliver with a comfortable place, without loss of time. This led to a more friendly and confidential dialogue; from which Oliver discovered that his friend's name was Jack Dawkins—among his intimate friends better known as the "Artful Dodger"—and that he was a peculiar pet and *protege* of the elderly gentleman before mentioned.

As John Dawkins objected to their entering London before nightfall, it was nearly eleven o'clock when they reached the small city street, along which the Dodger scudded at a rapid pace, directing Oliver to follow close at his heels.

Although Oliver had enough to occupy his attention in keeping sight of his leader, he could not help bestowing a few hasty glances on either side of the way as he passed along. A dirtier or more wretched place he had never seen.

Oliver was just considering whether he hadn't better run away, when they reached the bottom of the hill. His conductor, catching him by the arm, pushed open the door of a house, and, drawing him into the passage, closed it behind them.

"Now, then!" cried a voice from below, in reply to a whistle from the Dodger.

"Plummy and slam!" was the reply.

This seemed to be some watchword or signal that all was right; for the light of a feeble candle gleamed on the wall at the remote end of the passage, and a man's face peeped out from where a balustrade of the old kitchen staircase had been broken away.

"There's two on you," said the man, thrusting the candle farther out, and shading his eyes with his hand. "Who's the t'other one?"

"A new pal," replied Jack Dawkins, pulling Oliver forward.

"Where did he come from?"

"Greenland. Is Fagin upstairs?"

"Yes; he's a sortin' the wipes. Up with you!" The candle was drawn back, and the face disappeared.

Oliver, groping his way with one hand, and having the other firmly grasped by his companion, ascended with much difficulty the dark and broken stairs; which his conductor mounted with an ease and expedition that showed he was well acquainted with them. He threw open the door of a back-room, and drew Oliver in after him.

The walls and ceiling of the room were perfectly black with age and dirt. There was a deal table before the fire, upon which were a candle stuck in a ginger-beer bottle, two or three pewter-pots, a loaf and butter, and a plate. Seated round the table were four or five boys, none older than the Dodger, smoking long clay pipes and drinking spirits, with the air of middle-aged men. These all crowded about their associate as he whispered a few words to the Jewish proprietor; and then turned round and grinned at Oliver. So did the Jew himself, toasting-fork in hand.

"This is him, Fagin," said Jack Dawkins; "my friend, Oliver Twist."

The Jew grinned, and, making a low obeisance to Oliver, took him by the hand, and hoped he should have the honor of his intimate acquaintance. Upon this, the young gentlemen with the pipes came round him and shook both his hands very hard.

"We are very glad to see you, Oliver, very," said the Jew. "Dodger, take off the sausages, and draw a tub near the fire for Oliver. Ah! you're a-staring at the pocket-handkerchiefs! eh, my dear! There are a good many of 'em, ain't there? We've just looked 'em out, ready for the wash: that's all, Oliver—that's all. Ha! ha! ha!"

The latter part of this speech was hailed by a boisterous shout from all the pupils of the merry old gentleman; in the midst of which they went to supper.

Oliver ate his share, and the Jew then mixed him a glass of hot gin and water, telling him he must drink it off directly, because another gentleman wanted the tumbler. Oliver did as he was desired. Immediately afterward he felt himself gently lifted on to one of the sacks; and then he sunk into a deep sleep.

It was late next morning when Oliver awoke from a sound, long sleep. There was no other person in the room but the old Jew, who was boiling some coffee in a saucepan for breakfast, and whistling softly to himself as he stirred it round and round with an iron spoon. He would stop every now and then to listen when there was the least noise below; and when he had satisfied himself, he would go on, whistling and stirring again, as before.

Although Oliver had roused himself from sleep, he was not thoroughly awake.

Oliver was precisely in this condition. He saw the Jew with his

FAGIN

half-closed eyes; heard his low whistling; and recognized the sound of the spoon grating against the saucepan's sides.

When the coffee was done, the Jew drew the saucepan to the hob, looked at Oliver, and called him by his name. He did not answer, and was to all appearance asleep.

After satisfying himself upon this head, the Jew stepped gently to the door, which he fastened. He then drew forth, as it seemed to Oliver, from some trap in the floor, a small box, which he placed carefully on the table. His eyes glistened as he raised the lid and looked in. Dragging an old chair to the table, he sat down; and took from it a magnificent gold watch, sparkling with jewels.

"Aha!" said the Jew, shrugging up his shoulders and distorting every feature with a hideous grin. "Clever dogs! Clever dogs! Stanch to the last! Never told the old parson where they were. Never peached upon old Fagin! And why should they? It wouldn't have loosened the knot, or kept the drop up, a minute longer. No, no, no! Fine fellows! Fine fellows!"

With these and other muttered reflections of the like nature, the Jew once more deposited the watch in its place of safety. At least half a dozen more were severally drawn forth from the same box, and surveyed with equal pleasure; besides rings, bracelets, and other articles of jewelry, of such magnificent materials, and costly workmanship, that Oliver had no idea even of their names.

As the Jew looked up, his bright dark eyes, which had been staring at the jewelry, fell on Oliver's face; the boy's eyes were fixed on his in mute curiosity; and although the recognition was only for an instant, it was enough to show the old man that he had been observed. He closed the lid of the box with a loud crash; and, laying his hand on a bread-knife which was on the table, started furiously up.

"What's that?" said the Jew. "What do you watch me for? Why are you awake? What have you seen? Speak out boy! Quick—quick! for your life!"

"I wasn't able to sleep any longer, sir," replied Oliver, meekly. "I am very sorry if I have disturbed you, sir."

"You were not awake an hour ago?" said the Jew, scowling fiercely.

"No! No, indeed!" replied Oliver.

"Are you sure?" cried the Jew, with a still fiercer look than before, and a threatening attitude.

"Upon my word I was not, sir," replied Oliver, earnestly.

"Tush, tush, my dear!" said the Jew, abruptly resuming his old manner, and playing with the knife a little, before he laid it down; to make Oliver think that he had caught it up in mere sport. "Of course I know that, my dear. I only tried to frighten you. You're a brave boy. Ha! ha! you're a brave boy, Oliver!" The Jew rubbed his hands with a chuckle, but glanced uneasily at the box, notwithstanding.

"Did you see any of these pretty things, my dear?" said the Jew, laying his hand upon it after a short pause.

"Yes, sir," replied Oliver.

"Ah!" said the Jew, turning rather pale. "They—they're mine, Oliver; my little property. All I have to live upon in my old age. The folks call me a miser, my dear. Only a miser; that's all."

Oliver thought the old gentleman must be a decided miser to live in such a dirty place, with so many watches; but, thinking that perhaps his fondness for the Dodger and the other boys cost him a good deal of money, he only looked kindly at the Jew, and asked if he might get up.

"Certainly, my dear, certainly," replied the old gentleman. "There's a pitcher of water in the corner by the door. Bring it here, and I'll give you a basin to wash in, my dear."

Oliver got up, walked across the room, and stooped for an instant to raise the pitcher. When he turned his head the box was gone.

He had scarcely washed himself, and made everything tidy by emptying the basin out of the window, agreeably to the Jew's directions, when the Dodger returned, accompanied by a very sprightly young friend, whom Oliver had seen smoking on the previous night, and who was now formally introduced to him as Charley Bates. The four sat down to breakfast on the coffee and some hot rolls and ham which the Dodger had brought home in the crown of his hat.

"Well," said the Jew, glancing slyly at Oliver, and addressing himself to the Dodger, "I hope you've been at work this morning, my dears?"

"Hard," replied the Dodger.

"As nails," added Charley Bates.

"Good boys, good boys!" said the Jew. "What have *you*, Dodger?"

"A couple of pocket-books," replied that young gentleman.

"Lined?" inquired the Jew, with eagerness.

"Pretty well," replied the Dodger, producing two pocket-books.

"Not so heavy as they might be," said the Jew, after looking at the insides carefully; "but very neat and nicely made. Ingenious workman, ain't he, Oliver?"

"Very, indeed, sir," said Oliver. At which Mr. Charles Bates laughed uproariously, very much to the amazement of Oliver, who saw nothing to laugh at in anything that had passed.

"And what have you got, my dear?" said Fagin to Charley Bates.

"Wipes," replied Master Bates; at the same time producing four pocket-handkerchiefs.

"Well," said the Jew, inspecting them closely; "they're very good ones; very. You haven't marked them well, though, Charley; so the marks shall be picked out with a needle, and we'll teach Oliver how to do it. Shall us, Oliver, eh? Ha! ha! ha!"

"If you please, sir," said Oliver.

"You'd like to be able to make pocket-handkerchiefs as easy as Charley Bates, wouldn't you, my dear?" said the Jew.

"Very much, indeed, if you'll teach me, sir," replied Oliver.

Master Bates burst into another laugh.

"He is so jolly green!" said Charley when he recovered, as an apology to the company for his unpolite behavior.

The Dodger said nothing, but he smoothed Oliver's hair over his eyes, and said he'd know better by-and-by.

When the breakfast was cleared away, the merry old gentleman and the two boys played at a very curious and uncommon game, which was performed in this way: The merry old gentleman, placing a snuff-box in one pocket of his trousers, a note-case in the other, and a watch in his waistcoat pocket, with a guard-chain round his neck, and sticking a mock-diamond pin in his shirt, buttoned his coat tight around him, and putting his spectacle-case and handkerchief in his pockets, trotted up and down the room with a stick, in imitation of the manner in which old gentlemen walk about the streets any hour in the day.

Now during all this time the two boys followed him closely about, getting out of his sight, so nimbly, every time he turned round that it was impossible to follow their motions. At last the Dodger trod upon his toes or ran upon his boot accidentally, while Charley Bates stumbled up against him behind; and in that one moment they took from him, with the most extraordinary rapidity, snuff-box, note-case, watch-guard, chain, shirt-pin, pocket handkerchief, even the spectacle-case. If the old gentleman felt a hand in any one of his pockets, he cried out where it was, and then the game began all over again.

When this game had been played a great many times, Charley Bates expressed his opinion that it was time to pad the hoof. This, it occurred to Oliver, must be French for going out; for, directly afterward, the Dodger and Charley went away together, having been kindly furnished by the amiable old Jew with money to spend.

"There, my dear," said Fagin. "That's a pleasant life, isn't it? They have gone out for the day."

"Have they done work, sir?" inquired Oliver.

"Yes," said the Jew; "that is, unless they should unexpectedly come across any when they are out; and they won't neglect it, if they do, my dear, depend upon it. Make 'em your models, my dear. Make 'em your models," tapping the fire-shovel on the hearth to add force to his words: "do everything they bid you, and take their advice in all matters—especially the Dodger's, my dear. He'll be a great man himself, and will make you one too, if you take pattern by him. Is my handkerchief hanging out of my pocket, my dear?" said the Jew, stopping short.

"Yes, sir," said Oliver.

"See if you can take it out, without my feeling it, as you saw them do when we were at play this morning."

Oliver held up the bottom of the pocket with one hand, as he had seen the Dodger hold it, and drew the handkerchief lightly out with the other.

"Is it gone?" cried the Jew.

"Here it is, sir," said Oliver, showing it in his hand.

"You're a clever boy, my dear," said the playful old gentleman, patting Oliver on the head approvingly. "I never saw a sharper lad. Here's a shilling for you. If you go on in this way, you'll be the greatest man of the time. And now come here, and I'll show you how to take the marks out of the handkerchief."·

Oliver wondered what picking the old gentleman's pocket in play had to do with his chances of being a great man. But, thinking that the Jew, being so much his senior, must know best, he followed him quietly to the table, and was soon deeply involved in his new study.

For many days Oliver remained in the Jew's room, picking the marks out of the pocket-handkerchiefs (of which a great number were brought home), and sometimes taking part in the game already described, which the two boys and the Jew played, regularly, every morning.

At length, one morning, Oliver obtained the permission to go out with the boys. There had been no handkerchiefs to work upon for two or three days, and the dinners had been rather meagre. Perhaps these were reasons for the old gentleman giving his assent; but, whether they were or no, he told Oliver he might go, and placed him under the joint guardianship of Charley Bates and his friend the Dodger.

The three boys started out; the Dodger with his coat-sleeves tucked up and his hat cocked, as usual; Master Bates sauntering along with his hands in his pockets; and Oliver between them, wondering where they were going, and what they would teach him to make first.

They were just coming from a narrow court not far from an open square, which is yet called "The Green," when the Dodger made a sudden stop, and, laying his finger on his lip, drew his companions back again, with the greatest caution.

"What's the matter?" demanded Oliver.

"Hush!" replied the Dodger. "Do you see that old cove at the bookstall?"

"The old gentleman over the way?" said Oliver. "Yes, I see him."

"He'll do," said the Dodger.

"A prime plant," observed Master Charley Bates.

Oliver looked from one to the other with the greatest surprise, but he was not permitted to make any inquiries; for the two boys walked stealthily across the road and slunk close behind the old gentleman. Oliver walked a few paces after them, and, not knowing whether to advance or retire, stood looking on in silent amazement.

The old gentleman was a very respectable-looking personage, with a powdered head and gold spectacles, as he stood reading a book; and what was Oliver's horror and alarm as he stood a few paces off, looking on with his eyelids as wide open as they would possibly go, to see the

Dodger plunge his hand into the old gentleman's pocket and draw from thence a handkerchief! To see him hand the same to Charley Bates; and finally to behold them both running away round the corner.

In an instant the whole mystery of the handkerchiefs, and the watches, and the jewels, and the Jew, rushed upon the boy's mind. He stood, for a moment, with the blood so tingling through all his veins from terror that he felt as if he were in a burning fire; then, confused and frightened, he took to his heels, and, not knowing what he did, made off as fast as he could lay his feet to the ground.

This was all done in a minute's space. In the very instant when Oliver began to run, the old gentleman, putting his hand to his pocket, and missing his handkerchief, turned sharp round. Seeing the boy scudding away at such a rapid pace, he very naturally concluded him to be the thief; and, shouting "Stop thief!" with all his might, made off after him, book in hand.

But the old gentleman was not the only person who raised the hue-and-cry. The Dodger and Master Bates, unwilling to attract public attention by running down the open street, had merely retired into the very first doorway round the corner. They no sooner heard the cry, and saw Oliver running, than, guessing exactly how the matter stood, they issued forth with great promptitude; and shouting "Stop thief!" too, joined in the pursuit like good citizens.

Away they run, pell-mell, helter-skelter, slap-dash: tearing, yelling, screaming, knocking down the passengers as they turn the corners, rousing up the dogs, and astonishing the fowls; and making streets, squares, and courts re-echo with the sound.

At last a burly fellow struck Oliver a terrible blow and he went down upon the pavement; and the crowd eagerly gathered round him, each newcomer jostling and struggling with the others to catch a glimpse. "Stand aside!" "Give him a little air!" "Nonsense! he don't deserve it!" "Where's the gentleman?" "Here he is, coming down the street." "Make room there for the gentleman!" "Is this the boy, sir?"

Oliver lay, covered with mud and dust, and bleeding from the mouth, looking wildly round upon the heap of faces that surrounded him, when the old gentleman was officiously dragged and pushed into the circle by the foremost of the pursurers.

"Yes," said the gentleman, "I am afraid it is the boy."

"Afraid!" murmured the crowd. "That's a good 'un!"

"Poor fellow!" said the gentleman, "he has hurt himself."

"I did that, sir," said a great lubberly fellow, stepping forward; "and preciously I cut my knuckle agin his mouth. I stopped him, sir,"

The fellow touched his hat with a grin, expecting something for his pains; but the old gentleman, eyeing him with an expression of dislike, looked anxiously round, as if he contemplated running away himself: which it is very possible he might have attempted to do, and thus have afforded another chase, had not a police officer (who is generally the last person to arrive in such cases) at that moment made his way through the crowd, and seized Oliver by the collar.

"Come, get up," said the man, roughly.

"It wasn't me, indeed, sir. Indeed, indeed, it was two other boys," said Oliver, clasping his hands passionately and looking round. "They are here somewhere."

"Oh no, they ain't," said the officer. He meant this to be ironical, but it was true besides; for the Dodger and Charley Bates had filed off down the first convenient court they came to. "Come, get up!"

"Don't hurt him," said the old gentleman, compassionately.

"Oh no, I won't hurt him," replied the officer, tearing his jacket half off his back, in proof thereof. "Come, I know you; it won't do. Will you stand upon your legs, you young devil?"

Oliver, who could hardly stand, made a shift to raise himself on his feet, and was at once lugged along the streets by the jacket-collar at a rapid pace. The gentleman walked on with them by the officer's side.

At last they came to a place called Mutton Hill. Here he was led beneath a low archway, and up a dirty court, where they saw a stout man with a bunch of whiskers on his face and a bunch of keys in his hand.

"What's the matter now?" said the man carelessly.

"A young fogle-hunter," replied the officer who had Oliver in charge.

"Are you the party that's been robbed, sir?" inquired the man with the keys.

"Yes, I am," replied the old gentleman; "but I am not sure that this boy actually took the handkerchief. I would rather not press the case."

"Must go before the magistrate now, sir," replied the man. "His worship will be disengaged in half a minute. Now, young gallows!"

This was an invitation for Oliver to enter through a door which he unlocked as he spoke, and which led into a stone cell. Here he was searched, and, nothing being found upon him, locked up.

The old gentleman looked almost as unhappy as Oliver when the key grated in the lock.

At last Mr. Brownlow was summoned before the magistrate—a very mean man, whose name was Fang. Oliver was brought in, and the magistrate, after using very abusive language to Mr. Brownlow, had him sworn, but would not let him tell his story. He flew into a rage and told the policeman to tell what happened.

The policeman, with becoming humility, related how he had taken the boy; how he had searched Oliver, and found nothing on his person; and how that was all he knew about it.

"Are there any witnesses?" inquired Mr. Fang.

"None, your worship," replied the policeman.

Mr. Fang sat silent for some minutes, and then, turning round to Mr. Brownlow, said in a towering passion:

"Do you mean to state what your complaint against this boy is, man, or do you not? You have been sworn. Now, if you stand there, refusing to give evidence, I'll punish you for disrespect to the bench."

With many interruptions, and repeated insults, Mr. Brownlow contrived to state his case; observing that, in the surprise of the moment, he had run after the boy because he saw him running away.

"He has been hurt already," said the old gentleman, in conclusion. "And I fear," he added, with great energy, looking toward the bar, "I really fear that he is ill."

"Oh! yes, I dare say!" said Mr. Fang, with a sneer. "Come, none of your tricks here, you young vagabond; they won't do. What's your name?"

Oliver tried to reply, but his tongue failed him. He was deadly pale; and the whole place seemed turning round and round.

"What's your name, you hardened scoundrel?" demanded Mr. Fang.

At this point of the inquiry, Oliver raised his head, and, looking round with imploring eyes, asked feebly for a drink of water.

"Stuff and nonsense!" said Fang; "don't try to make a fool of me."

"I think he really is ill, your worship," remonstrated the officer.

"I know better," said Mr. Fang.

"Take care of him, officer," said the old gentleman, raising his hands instinctively; "he'll fall down."

"Stand away, officer," cried Fang; "let him, if he likes."

Oliver availed himself of the kind permission, and fell to the floor in a fainting fit. The men in the office looked at each other, but no one dared to stir.

"I knew he was shamming," said Fang, as if this were incontestable proof of the fact. "Let him lie there; he'll soon be tired of that."

"How do you propose to deal with the case, sir?" inquired the clerk in a low voice.

"Summarily," replied Mr. Fang. "He stands committed for three months—hard labor, of course. Clear the office."

The door was opened for this purpose, and a couple of men were preparing to carry the insensible boy to his cell, when an elderly man of decent but poor appearance, clad in an old suit of black, rushed in.

"Stop! stop! Don't take him away! For heaven's sake stop a moment!" cried the newcomer, breathless with haste.

"What is this? Who is this? Turn this man out. Clear the office," cried Mr. Fang.

"I *will* speak," cried the man; "I will not be turned out. I saw it all. I keep the book-stall. I demand to be sworn. I will not be put down. Mr. Fang, you must hear me. You must not refuse, sir."

The man was right. His manner was determined; and the matter was growing rather too serious to be hushed up.

"Swear the man," growled Mr. Fang, with a very ill grace. "Now, man, what have you got to say?"

"This," said the man: "I saw three boys—two others and the prisoner here—loitering on the opposite side of the way, when this gentleman was reading. The robbery was committed by another boy. I saw it done; and I saw this boy was perfectly amazed and stupefied by it."

"Why didn't you come here before?" said Fang, after a pause.

"I hadn't a soul to mind the shop," replied the man. "Everybody who could have helped me had joined in the pursuit. I could get nobody till five minutes ago; and I have run here all the way to speak the truth."

"The boy is discharged. Clear the office!" shouted the irate magistrate.

The mandate was obeyed; and as Oliver was taken out he fainted away again in the yard, and lay with his face a deadly white and a cold tremble convulsing his frame.

"Poor boy! poor boy!" said Mr. Brownlow, bending over him. "Call a coach, somebody, pray. Directly!"

A coach was obtained, and Oliver, having been carefully laid on one seat, the old gentleman got in and sat himself on the other.

"May I accompany you?" said the book-stall keeper, looking in.

"Bless me, yes, my dear sir," said Mr. Brownlow quickly. "I forgot you. Dear, dear! I have this unhappy book still! Jump in. Poor fellow! There's no time to lose."

The book-stall keeper got into the coach, and it rattled away. It stopped at length before a neat house, in a quiet shady street. Here a bed was prepared, without loss of time, in which Mr. Brownlow saw his young charge carefully and comfortably deposited; and here he was tended with a kindness and solicitude that knew no bounds.

At last the sick boy began to recover, and one day Mr. Brownlow came in to see him. You may imagine how happy Oliver was to see his good benefactor; but he was no more delighted than was Mr. Brownlow. The old gentleman came to spend a short time with him every day; and, when he grew stronger, Oliver went up to the learned gentleman's study and talked with him by the hour and was astonished at the books he saw, and which Mr. Brownlow told him to look at and read as much as he liked.

Oliver was soon well, and no thought was in Mr. Brownlow's mind but that he should keep him, and raise him and educate him to be a splendid man; for no father loves his own son better than Mr. Brownlow had come to love Oliver.

Now, I know, you want to ask me what became of Oliver Twist. But I cannot tell you here. Let us leave him in this beautiful home of good Mr. Brownlow; and, if you want to read the rest of his wonderful story, get Dickens' big book called *Oliver Twist*, and read it there. There were many surprises and much trouble yet in store for Oliver, but he was **always noble, honest, and brave.**

MR. JINGLE.

"YOU have been in Spain, sir?" said Mr. Tracy Tupman.

"Lived there—ages."

"Many conquests, sir?" inquired Mr. Tupman.

"Conquests! Thousands. Don Bolaro Fizzgig—Grandee—only daughter—Donna Christina—splendid creature—loved me to distraction—jealous father—high-souled daughter—handsome Englishman—Donna Christina in despair—prussic acid—stomach pump in my portmanteau—operation performed—old Bolaro in ecstasies—consent to our union—join hands and floods of tears—romantic story very."

"Is the lady in England now, sir?" inquired Mr. Tupman, on whom the description of her charms had produced a powerful impression.

"Dead, sir—dead," said the stranger, applying to his right eye the brief remnant of a very old cambric handkerchief. "Never recovered the stomach pump—undermined constitution—fell a victim."

"And her father?" inquired the poetic Snodgrass.

"Remorse and misery," replied the stranger. "Sudden disappearance—talk of the whole city—search made everywhere—without success—public fountain in the great square suddenly ceased playing—weeks elapsed—still a stoppage—workmen employed to clean it—water drawn off—father-in-law discovered sticking head first in the main pipe, with a full confession in his right boot—took him out, and the fountain played away again, as well as ever."

"Will you allow me to note that little romance down, sir?" said Mr. Snodgrass, deeply affected.

"Certainly, sir, certainly—fifty more if you like to hear 'em—strange life mine—rather curious history—not extraordinary, but singular."

In this strain, with an occasional glass of ale, by way of parenthesis, when the coach changed horses, did the stranger proceed, until they reached Rochester bridge, by which time the note-books, both of Mr. Pickwick and Mr. Snodgrass, were completely filled with selections from his adventures.

Pickwick Papers.

POOR JO.

*H*ERE'S the boy, gentlemen!

Here he is, very muddy, very hoarse, very ragged.

Name, Jo. Nothing else that he knows on. Don't know that everybody has two names. Never heerd of sich a think. Don't know that Jo is short for a longer name. Thinks it long enough for *him*. *He* don't find no fault with it. Spell it? No. *He* can't spell it. No father, no mother, no friends. Never been to school. What's home? Knows a broom's a broom, and knows it's wicked to tell a lie. Don't recollect who told him about the broom, or about the lie, but knows both. Can't exactly say what'll be done to him after he's dead if he tells a lie to the gentlemen here, but believes it'll be something wery bad to punish him, and serve him right—and so he'll tell the truth.

Bleak House.

SAM AND MARY THE HOUSEMAID.

"*H*OW de do, sir?" said Mr. Muzzle, as he conducted Mr. Weller down the kitchen stairs.

"Why, no considerable change has taken place in the state of my system, since I see you cocked up behind your Governor's chair in the parlour, a little vile ago," replied Sam.

"You will excuse my not taking any notice of you then," said Mr. Muzzle. "You see, master hadn't introduced us, then. Lord, how fond he is of you, Mr. Weller, to be sure!"

"Ah!" said Sam, "what a pleasant chap he is!"

"Ain't he?" replied Mr. Muzzle.

"So much humour," said Sam.

"And such a man to speak," said Mr. Muzzle. "How his ideas flow, don't they?"

"Wonderful," replied Sam; "they comes a pouring out, knocking each other's heads so fast, that they seems to stun one another; you hardly know what he's arter, do you?"

"That's the great merit of his style of speaking," rejoined Mr. Muzzle. "Take care of the last step, Mr. Weller. Would you like to wash your hands, sir, before we join the ladies? Here's a sink, with the water laid on, sir, and a clean jack-towel behind the door."

"Ah! perhaps I may as well have a rinse," replied Mr. Weller, applying plenty of yellow soap to the towel, and rubbing away, till his face shone again. "How many ladies are there?"

"Only two in our kitchen," said Mr. Muzzle, "cook and 'ousemaid. We keep a boy to do the dirty work, and a gal besides, but they dine in the washus."

"Oh, they dines in the washus, do they?" said Mr. Weller.

"Yes," replied Mr. Muzzle, "we tried 'em at our table when they first come, but we couldn't keep 'em. The gal's manners is dreadful vulgar; and the boy breathes so very hard while he's eating, that we found it impossible to sit at table with him."

"Young grampus!" said Mr. Weller.

"Oh, dreadful," rejoined Mr. Muzzle; "but that is the worst of country service, Mr. Weller; the juniors is always so very savage. This way, sir, if you please; this way."

Preceding Mr. Weller, with the utmost politeness, Mr. Muzzle conducted him into the kitchen.

"Mary," said Mr. Muzzle to the pretty servant-girl, "this is Mr. Weller: a gentleman as master has sent down, to be made as comfortable as possible."

"And your master's a knowin' hand, and has just sent me to the right place," said Mr. Weller, with a glance of admiration at Mary. "If I wos

master o' this here house, I should alvays find the materials for comfort vere Mary wos."

"Lor', Mr. Weller!" said Mary, blushing.

"Well, I never!" ejaculated the cook.

"Bless me, cook, I forgot you," said Mr. Muzzle. "Mr. Weller, let me introduce you."

"How are you, ma'am?" said Mr. Weller. "Werry glad to see you, indeed, and hope our acquaintance may be a long 'un, as the gen'lm'n said to the fi'-pun'-note."

When this ceremony of introduction had been gone through, the cook and Mary retired into the back kitchen to titter, for ten minutes; then returning, all giggles and blushes, they sat down to dinner.

Mr. Weller's easy manners and conversational powers had such irresistible influence with his new friends, that before the dinner was half over, they were on a footing of perfect intimacy, and in possession of a full account of the delinquency of Job Trotter.

"I never could a-bear that Job," said Mary.

"No more you never ought to, my dear," replied Mr. Weller.

"Why not!" inquired Mary.

"Cos ugliness and svindlin' never ought to be formiliar with elegance and wirtew," replied Mr. Weller. "Ought they, Mr. Muzzle?"

"Not by no means," replied that gentleman.

Here Mary laughed, and said the cook had made her; and the cook laughed, and said she hadn't.

"I han't got a glass," said Mary.

"WERRY GLAD TO SEE YOU INDEED"

"CHOPS! GRACIOUS HEAVENS! AND TOMATO SAUCE!"

"Drink with me, my dear," said Mr. Weller. "Put your lips to this here tumbler, and then I can kiss you by deputy."

"For shame, Mr. Weller!" said Mary.

"What's a shame, my dear?"

"Talkin' in that way."

"Nosense; it ain't no harm. It's natur; ain't it, cook?"

"Don't ask me, imperence," replied the cook in a high state of delight: and hereupon the cook and Mary laughed again, till what between the beer, and the cold meat, and the laughter combined, the latter young lady was brought to the verge of choking—an alarming crisis from which she was only recovered by sundry pats on the back, and other necessary attentions, most delicately administered by Mr. Samuel Weller. *Pickwick Papers.*

DICK SWIVELLER AND THE MARCHIONESS.

RICHARD SWIVELLER, being often left alone, began to find the time hang heavy on his hands. For the better preservation of his cheerfulness therefore, and to prevent his faculties from rusting, he provided himself with a cribbage-board and pack of cards, and accustomed himself to play at cribbage with a dummy, for twenty, thirty, or sometimes even fifty thousand pounds a side, besides many hazardous bets to a considerable amount.

As these games were very silently conducted, notwithstanding the magnitude of the interests involved, Mr. Swiveller began to think that on those evenings when Mr. and Miss Brass were out (and they often went out now) he heard a kind of snorting or hard-breathing sound in the direction of the door, which it occurred to him, after some reflection, must proceed from the small servant, who always had a cold from damp living. Looking intently that way one night, he plainly distinguished an eye gleaming and glistening at the keyhole; and having now no doubt that his suspicions were correct, he stole softly to the door, and pounced upon her before she was aware of his approach.

"Oh! I didn't mean any harm indeed, upon my word I didn't," cried the small servant, struggling like a much larger one. "It's so very dull, downstairs. Please don't you tell upon me, please don't."

"Tell upon you!" said Dick. "Do you mean to say you were looking through the keyhole for company?"

"Yes, upon my word I was," replied the small servant.

"How long have you been cooling your eye there?" said Dick.

"Oh, ever since you first began to play them cards, and long before."

"Well—come in,"—he said, after a little consideration. "Here—sit down, and I'll teach you how to play."

"Oh! I durstn't do it," rejoined the small servant; "Miss Sally 'ud kill me if she know'd I came up here."

"Have you got a fire downstairs?" said Dick.

"A very little one," replied the small servant.

"Miss Sally couldn't kill me if she know'd I went down there, so I'll come," said Richard, putting the cards into his pocket. "Why, how thin you are! What do you mean by it?"

"It an't my fault."

"Could you eat any bread and meat?" said Dick, taking down his hat. "Yes! Ah! I thought so. Did you ever taste beer?"

"I had a sip of it once," said the small servant.

"Here's a state of things!" cried Mr. Swiveller, raising his eyes to the ceiling. "She *never* tasted it—it can't be tasted in a sip! Why, how old are you?"

"I don't know."

Mr. Swiveller opened his eyes very wide, and appeared thoughtful for a moment; then, bidding the child mind the door until he came back, vanished straightway.

Presently, he returned, followed by the boy from the public-house, who bore in one hand a plate of bread and beef, and in the other a great pot, filled with some very fragrant compound, which sent forth a grateful steam, and was indeed choice purl, made after a particular recipe which

DICK SWIVELLER AND THE MARCHIONESS.

Mr. Swiveller had imparted to the landlord, at a period when he was deep in his books and desirous to conciliate his friendship. Relieving the boy of his burden at the door, and charging his little companion to fasten it to prevent surprise, Mr. Swiveller followed her into the kitchen.

"There!" said Richard, putting the plate before her. "First of all clear that off, and then you'll see what's next."

The small servant needed no second bidding, and the plate was soon empty.

"Next," said Dick, handing the purl, "take a pull at that; but moderate your transports, you know, for you're not used to it. Well, is it good?"

"Oh! isn't it?" said the small servant.

Mr. Swiveller appeared gratified beyond all expression by this reply, and took a long draught himself: steadfastly regarding his companion while he did so. These preliminaries disposed of, he applied himself to teaching her the game, which she soon learnt tolerably well, being both sharp-witted and cunning.

"Now," said Mr. Swiveller, putting two sixpences into a saucer, and trimming the wretched candle, when the cards had been cut and dealt, "those are the stakes. If you win, you get 'em all. If I win, I get 'em. To make it seem more real and pleasant, I shall call you the Marchioness, do you hear?"

The small servant nodded.

"Then, Marchioness," said Mr. Swiveller, "fire away!"

The Marchioness, holding her cards very tight in both hands, considered which to play, and Mr. Swiveller, assuming the gay and fashionable air which such society required, took another pull at the tankard, and waited for her lead.

Mr. Swiveller and his partner played several rubbers with varying success, until the loss of three sixpences, the gradual sinking of the purl, and the striking of ten o'clock, combined to render that gentleman mindful of the flight of Time, and the expediency of withdrawing before Mr. Sampson and Miss Sally Brass returned.

Old Curiosity Shop.

THE MEANING OF "CHOPS AND TOMATO SAUCE."

ND now, gentlemen, but one word more. Two letters have passed between these parties, letters which are admitted to be in the hand-writing of the defendant, and which speak volumes, indeed. These letters, too, bespeak the character of the man. They are not open, fervent, eloquent epistles, breathing nothing but the language of affectionate attachment. They are covert, sly, underhanded communications, but, fortunately, far more conclusive than if couched in the most glowing language and the most poetic imagery—letters that must be viewed with a cautious and suspicious eye—letters that were evidently intended at the time, by Pickwick, to mislead and delude any third parties into whose hands they might fall. Let me read the first:— "Garraway's, twelve o'clock. Dear Mrs. B.—Chops and Tomato sauce. Yours, Pickwick." Gentlemen, what does this mean? Chops and Tomata sauce. Yours, Pickwick! Chops! Gracious Heavens! and Tomato sauce! Gentlemen, is the happiness of a sensitive and confiding female to be trifled away, by such shallow artifices as these? The next has no date whatever, which is in itself suspicious. "Dear Mrs. B., I shall not be at home till to-morrow. Slow coach." And then follows this very remarkable expression. "Don't trouble yourself about the warming pan."  The warming pan! Why, gentlemen, who *does* trouble himself about a warming-pan! When was the peace of mind of man or woman broken or disturbed by a warming-pan, which is in itself a harmless, a useful, and I will add, gentlemen, a comforting article of domestic furniture? Why is Mrs. Bardell so earnestly entreated not to agitate herself about this warming-pan, unless (as is no doubt the case) it is a mere cover for hidden fire?

Pickwick Papers.

MR. MICAWBER GIVES ADVICE.

MR. MICAWBER was waiting for me within the gate, and we went up to his room (top story but one), and cried very much. He solemnly conjured me, I remember, to take warning by his fate; and to observe that if a man had twenty pounds a-year for his income, and spent nineteen pounds nineteen shillings and sixpence, he would be happy, but that if he spent twenty pounds one he would be miserable. After which he borrowed a shilling of me for porter, gave me a written order on Mrs. Micawber for the amount, and put away his pocket-handkerchief, and cheered up.

David Copperfield.

A MISUNDERSTANDING BETWEEN TWO PICKWICKIANS.

MR. PICKWICK took up his hat, and repaired to the Peacock, but Mr. Winkle had conveyed the intelligence of the fancy ball there, before him.

"Mrs. Pott's going," were the first words with which he saluted his leader.

"Is she?" said Mr. Pickwick.

"As Apollo," replied Winkle. "Only Pott objects to the tunic."

"He is right. He is quite right," said Mr. Pickwick emphatically.

"Yes;—so she's going to wear a white satin gown with gold spangles."

"They'll hardly know what she's meant for; will they?" inquired Mr. Snodgrass.

"Of course they will," replied Mr. Winkle indignantly. "They'll see her lyre, won't they?"

A MISUNDERSTANDING.

"True ; I forgot that," said Mr. Snodgrass.

"I shall go as a Bandit," interposed Mr. Tupman.

"What !" said Mr. Pickwick, with a sudden start.

"As a Bandit," repeated Mr. Tupman mildly.

"You don't mean to say," said Mr. Pickwick, gazing with solemn sternness at his friend, "you don't mean to say, Mr. Tupman, that it is your intention to put yourself into a green velvet jacket with a two-inch tail ?"

"Such *is* my intention, sir," replied Mr. Tupman warmly. "And why not, sir ?"

"Because, sir," said Mr. Pickwick, considerably excited, "because you are too old, sir."

"Too old !" exclaimed Mr. Tupman.

"And if any further ground of objection be wanting," continued Mr. Pickwick, "you are too fat, sir."

"Sir," said Mr. Tupman, his face suffused with a crimson glow. "This is an insult."

"Sir," replied Mr. Pickwick in the same tone, "it is not half the insult to you, that your appearance in my presence in a green velvet jacket, with a two-inch tail, would be to me."

"Sir," said Mr. Tupman, "you're a fellow."

"Sir," said Mr. Pickwick, "you're another !"

Mr. Tupman advanced a step or two, and glared at Mr. Pickwick. Mr. Pickwick returned the glare, concentrated into a focus by means of his spectacles, and breathed a bold defiance. Mr. Snodgrass and Mr. Winkle looked on, petrified at beholding such a scene between two such men.

"Sir," said Mr. Tupman, after a short pause, speaking in a low, deep voice, "you have called me old."

"I have," said Mr. Pickwick.

"And fat."

"I reiterate the charge."

"And a fellow."

"So you are !"

There was a fearful pause.